THE COMPLETE
BOOK OF
BAYERN
MUNICH

VERLAG DIE WERKSTATT

The author

Christoph Bausenwein has published several highly respected books with Verlag Die Werkstatt, most recently about German national coach Joachim Löw and Uli Hoeness, Bayern Munich president and former player. He has also written several children's books on football.

Photo credits

firo sportphoto: 64, 65b, 72b, 73 (2), 74l, 75 (4), 76l, 97t, 102b

Fotoagentur Horst Müller: Cover (5), 6b (4), 8br, 9, 19t, 22 (5), 23, 25tl, 26 (2), 29, 31 (3), 32, 33r, 34 (2), 35 (2), 36 (4), 37, 38l, 39tr, 40r, 41b, 42, 43 (8), 44b, 45t, 47, 48, 49 (8), 50 (3), 52t, 53t, 54 (2), 55 (2), 56 (2), 57t, 58 (2), 63t, 64b, 72t, 73b, 78 (2), 83t, 84/85, 88b, 91tr, 93, 95b, 96 (2), 97b, 98b, 101t, 103m, 104t, 105 (2)

Getty Images: 6t, 51, 53b, 79, 86b, 94

Imago Sportfoto: Cover (2, Schweinsteiger, Scholl), reverse side, endpaper, 5, 24 (2), 25tr, 27, 28, 30, 40l, 41t, 52b, 58 (stadium), 63b, 68 (2), 69 (2), 70 (2), 71 (2), 73 (Dante), 74r, 76r, 77 (3), 78b (2), 87m, 89t, 91tl, 96b, 100, 101b, 107

picture alliance/dpa: Cover (Müller), 2/3, 33t, 38r, 43 (Aumann), 44t, 45b, 46, 50bl, 55b, 57b, 58r, 59 (2), 59tl+tm, 60 (2), 61 (4), 62, 65t, 66, 67 (3), 77tl, 78 (children), 80 (2), 81 (2), 85b, 87 (2), 89b, 90b, 91b, 92, 95t, 103b, 106

Andreas Kalka: 39u; autor's archive: 17 (4), 20, 21r (6), 105t; Bildarchiv Preußischer Kulturbesitz: 12, FC Bayern Munich: 85t; Herbert Liedel: 36b, 39tl; Historisches Sportarchiv Wolfram Dietz: 17t (3), 102, 103t, 104b; private archive of Uri Siegel: 90t; Martin Schölkopf: 99; Stadtarchiv München: 82b; Thilo Thielke: 86t

Remaining photos: Publisher's archive

Bibliographic information of the Deutsche Nationalbibliothek: the Deutsche Nationalbibliothek lists this publication in the Deutsche Nationalbibliografie; detailed bibliographic data are available on the Internet at http://dnb.d-nb.de.

Copyright © 2013 Verlag Die Werkstatt GmbH
Lotzestrasse 22a, D-37083 Göttingen
www.werkstatt-verlag.de
All rights reserved.
Translated from German by Wendy Brouwer
Typesetting and design: Verlag Die Werkstatt
Cover design: www.vogelsangdesign.de
Printing and binding: aprinta-druck, Wemding

ISBN 978-3-7307-0061-7

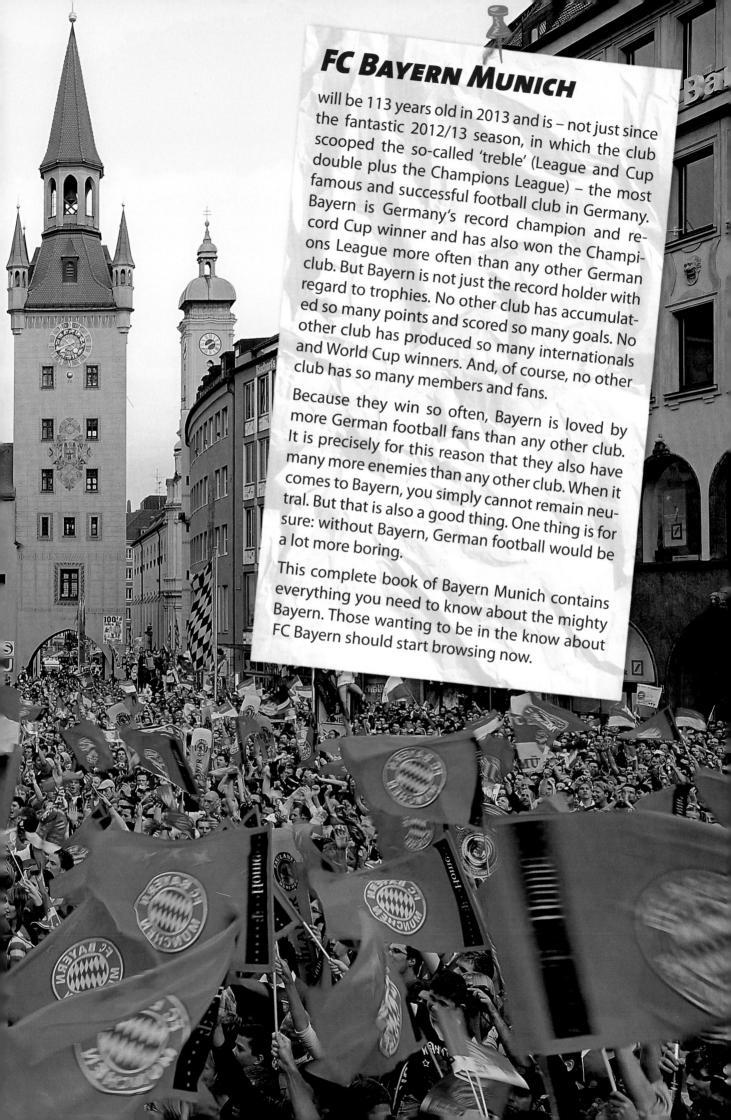

FC Bayern Munich

will be 113 years old in 2013 and is – not just since the fantastic 2012/13 season, in which the club scooped the so-called 'treble' (League and Cup double plus the Champions League) – the most famous and successful football club in Germany. Bayern is Germany's record champion and record Cup winner and has also won the Champions League more often than any other German club. But Bayern is not just the record holder with regard to trophies. No other club has accumulated so many points and scored so many goals. No other club has produced so many internationals and World Cup winners. And, of course, no other club has so many members and fans.

Because they win so often, Bayern is loved by more German football fans than any other club. It is precisely for this reason that they also have many more enemies than any other club. When it comes to Bayern, you simply cannot remain neutral. But that is also a good thing. One thing is for sure: without Bayern, German football would be a lot more boring.

This complete book of Bayern Munich contains everything you need to know about the mighty Bayern. Those wanting to be in the know about FC Bayern should start browsing now.

CONTENTS

2013: In the Bundesliga's 50th anniversary season, Bayern is crowned champion for the 23rd time.

BAYERN: THE RECORD CLUB

50 per cent chance of winning the league

As of 2013 Bayern has scooped 22 titles in 45 seasons since their first Bundesliga triumph in 1969. It means those tipping Bayern to win the championship before the season have a 50 per cent chance of being right!

Over all competitions FC Bayern is by far the most successful German football club. It has accumulated the most titles in the European cup competitions and the DFB-Pokal (the German FA cup) and even more notably is the number one club in the league. Since 1965 Bayern has competed in 1,636 Bundesliga games in 48 seasons. And even though they have played 60 fewer games than Hamburger SV (50 seasons), they nevertheless hold almost every record. Bayern leads not only on titles but also on points, goals, victories and winning streaks. And they have broken, or equalled, most of their records in the 2012/13 'super-season'. But what Germans call Bayern's 'winner gene' (an innate will to succeed) does not only become apparent when Bayern manage to lead the league from the first matchday to the last (which they have done five times so far). It also manifests itself when Bayern win the league in the last second of the final match, as they did in 2001. During that season, 2000/01, when they lost nine times, they even set the record for being the 'champions with the most defeats'.

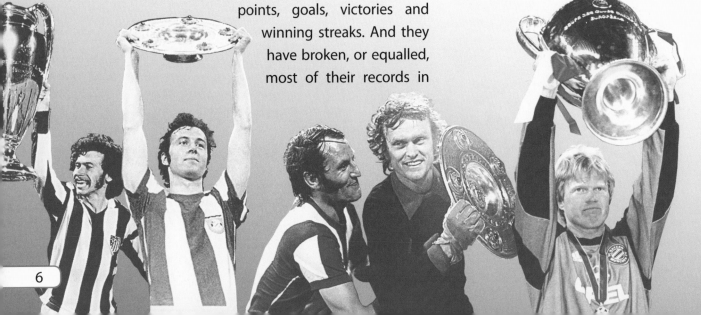

23 x German champion

1 x UEFA Cup winners

5 x European Cup / Champions League winner

16 x DFB-Pokal winner (9 doubles)

1 x Cup Winners' Cup victors

2 x Intercontinental Cup winners

Bundesliga records of FC Bayern

Total records (by 15.5.2013)*:
3510 Goals (goal difference +1,649)
3186 Points
936 Victories
626 Total matchdays spent in first place
600 Home wins
336 Away wins

Season records (where no date = 2012/13):
Biggest lead: **25 points**
Best second half of the season: **49 points**
Best goal difference: **+80**
Most points: **91**
Most victories in a season: **29**
Most goals in a season: **101** (1971/72)
Most clean sheets: **21**
Most home victories: **16** (1972/73, same as Schalke 1971/72 and Wolfsburg 2008/09)
Most away points: **47**
Most away victories: **15**
Fewest defeats: **1** (same as Bayern 1986/87)
Least goals against: **18**
Least away goals against: **7**
Least away defeats: **0** (same as Bayern 1986/87)
Earliest champions: **Matchday 28**

Longest winning streak: **14**
Longest winning streak away from home: **9**
Longest winning streak at the start of the season:
   8 victories

Runs over several seasons:
Longest winning streak: **15 victories** (19.3–20.9.2005)
Longest home winning streak: **26 victories**
   (27.11.1971–26.5.1973)
Consecutive home games undefeated: **73 games**
   (11.4.1970–14.9.1974)
Consecutive away games undefeated: **26 games**
   (14.12.1985–1.8.1987)
Longest scoring streak: **37 games** with at least one goal
   (21.4.2012–18.5.2013)

* FC Bayern lie in first place in the all-time Bundesliga table. In second place, by a large margin, is Werder Bremen (2,834 goals/goal difference +474, 2,564 points, 717 victories).

(Data up to the end of 2012/13 season European games include UEFA Super Cup and qualifying matches.)

Other records
400 games in Europe
218 wins in Europe
12 European finals

THE RED SHORTS FROM SCHWABING

FC Bayern 1900–1965

Bavarian champion
(Eastern District champion) 1910, 1911

Southern German champion
1926, 1928, 1932, 1965 (Regional League)

German champion 1932

DFB-Pokal winner 1957

FC Bayern in their founding year.

The Founding Of The Club

In 1895, the first footballers were seen on the area of land known as the Theresienwiese in Munich. However, there were not many football fans at first. Most young Germans preferred gymnastics. They were not keen on football because the game came from England and was therefore considered 'un-German'. Even when a lot of gymnastics clubs started their own football divisions, this changed very little. So those footballers who in 1897 joined MTV Munich (a men's gymnastics club) were still seen as outsiders – and all this at a time when highly paid professionals were already playing in front of tens of thousands in England.

Soon the footballers in the MTV were quarrelling among themselves. Some wanted football to only be supplemental to the gymnastics. The others wanted to ultimately play proper championship games in the Southern German Football Association, which had just been founded. 'We have to break the fetters of the gymnastic movement!' challenged the rebels through their ringleader Franz John. Hence on 7 February 1900 a meeting took place in the pub that doubled as MTV's clubhouse, the Bäckerhöfel, not far from the central square Marienplatz. At this gathering a vote was to be taken on whether MTV's football division should join the Southern German Football Association. When the gymnasts decided against it, eleven MTV footballers left the meeting out of protest. They proceeded to the inn called Gisela near another central square called Odeonsplatz and on that very same evening founded FC Bayern Munich as an independent club. Franz John was voted in as the first president.

Franz John, Bayern president 1900–1903, was, like so many members, not a genuine Bavarian.

The Name 'Bayern'

At the founding assembly the name of the new football club was discussed and it was finally decided to name the club after the German word for Bavaria – 'Bayern' (Germans put the letters FC in front of a club's name, that's why they say 'FC Bayern' instead of 'Bayern FC'.) In doing this they were following a widespread custom at the time. Many of the new football clubs emerging throughout Germany wanted to show pride in their homelands in the clubs' names. In the Rhineland or in Westphalia the clubs were called 'Rhenania' or 'Westfalia'; in and around Berlin there were many clubs calling themselves 'Preussen', or 'Borussia' (the Latin word for 'Prussia').

The First Games

The first official opponent of FC Bayern was the 1st Munich SC, in March 1900. Bayern reported for the game in pale blue jerseys and white shorts and won 5-2. A 7-1 triumph against their former club mates from MTV Munich followed soon after. Clubs that concentrated on football, so it seemed, were better at the game than clubs in which it was only a minor sport. No wonder that over the following years FC Bayern would be crowned Munich city champions several times.

'Newcomers'
Many of the founder members were not from Bavaria. Most of these men came from the state of Saxony and Northern Germany. Franz John, the first president in the club's history, came from Prinzwalk in the northeast, known today as Mecklenburg. It is not surprising that FC Bayern got the reputation of not really being a club of and for 'genuine' Bavarians, but rather for 'newcomers', from Prussia in the north.

The Dutchman Dr Willem Hesselink played with FC Bayern from 1903. He was the team's playmaker and also a fearsome goalscorer.

Red and White

The first club song was written to the melody of the Hymn of Bavaria (God be with you, land of the Bavarians):

We want to faithfully worship the sport,
To stand by it at any price,
We all want to faithfully swear only
By the colours: red and white!

GALLANTS FROM SCHWABING

FC Bayern was originally based in the district of Schwabing. The club's first home ground was on Clemensstrasse. In 1907 there followed a move to Leopoldstrasse, where a new sports ground, deemed ultramodern for its time, was available. At the time Schwabing was the centre for Munich's artists and students. Bayern was not a club for the working class, rather more for 'gallants', who put a great deal of value on education, good behaviour and chic clothing. Up until the First World War, everyone who wanted to be admitted into the club had to have at least attended a secondary school. Therefore members were above all students, artists and young business people. FC Bayern left Schwabing in 1946 in order to move to Säbener Strasse in the Harlaching area. However, the reputation of being a special club for the successful and prominent remained – for the 'in-crowd', so to speak.

THE RED SHORTS

Bayern originally played in pale blue shirts and white shorts. Out of practical considerations they then changed to white shirts and black shorts. After they briefly merged with the Munich Sports Club (MSC) in 1906 due to financial reasons, another change was ultimately made. The colour of the MSC, at the time the largest sports club in Munich, was red. Therefore from then on 'FC Bayern, football division of the MSC', played in white jerseys and red shorts. People soon referred to the players as the 'Reds' or the 'Red Shorts'. The players of the city's other big club, 1860 Munich, were correspondingly called the 'Blues'.

Around 1900, to the west of the English Garden, on Türkenstrasse in Schwabing, it was teeming with artists of all kinds.

Bayern is 1909/10 Eastern District champion.

THE FIRST SUCCESSES

In the 1907/08 season FC Bayern became regional champion of Upper Bavaria for the first time. In 1910 and 1911 the 'Reds' finally became state champions and lifted the Bavarian title (then also called the Eastern District Championship, because Bavaria was the eastern part of the Southern German Football Association). These successes above all rested on two courses of action: On the one hand, the club had already purposefully started signing promising talent. One the other, they had already been regularly playing the strong English professional teams for some time and were therefore constantly improving. The first successful Bayern team was coached by the Englishman Taylor; the best player was Max Gablonsky. This fast right winger was also Bayern's first international. In 1910 and 1911 he was capped four times.

Star signing

Before the 1910/11 season FC Bayern had purposefully bolstered the squad. The biggest star was goalkeeper Karl Pekarna. He came from Vienna and was renowned for his elegant flying saves. To entice this world-class man from local rivals FC Wacker Munich, Bayern had to pay a lot of money. Because at the time football in Germany was still purely a non-professional sport and no players were allowed to be paid, Pekarna was temporarily suspended by the Southern German FA.

The renowned Bayern goalkeeper Pekarna (left) in action.

Success With British Coaches

FC Bayern had been having positive experiences with coaches from the motherland of football since 1907. In the spring of 1919, the club acquired an outstanding football expert as their coach with the English ex-professional William Townley (Blackburn Rovers et al.), who in 1914 had led the team SpVgg Fürth to the German championship. Townley taught the Bayern players how to move upfield by stringing short passes together. This was not yet enough to win national titles, but nevertheless FC Bayern was now the best team in Southern Bavaria. When, in 1925, the Scot Jim McPherson took over the training, the 'Red Shorts' also learnt how to put in an effort and score goals in addition to playing. On 11 April 1926 Bayern secured the Southern German Championship with a 4-3 win in the final against SpVgg Fürth. Over the course of the season this 'wonder attack' from Munich had scored a legendary 176 goals!

In 1928 FC Bayern became Southern Germany champions for the second time.

Yet it was not enough for the first German Championship: in the knock-out rounds they were too certain of success and were defeated 2-0 by Fortuna Leipzig. (Until 1963, when the Bundesliga was formed, the German championship was decided through knock-out rounds contested by the various regional champions and then a final between the two surviving teams.)

1932: The First Championship

After two more failures in the final rounds, the time had finally come, under new coach Richard 'Little' Dombi, a Viennese man of Jewish-Hungarian descent: FC Bayern won the German championship! Even though local rivals Wacker Munich and 1860 Munich were also among the best teams in the country, Bayern prevailed because they could not only play, run, fight and

score goals – they now also knew how to defend. Based on a solid backline, the team built from the rear calmly and purposefully. In the semi-final, calm and composed Bayern eliminated the then footballing superpower FC Nuremberg (2-0), and the final, which took place in Nuremberg, produced a well-deserved 2-0 win against Eintracht Frankfurt. The striker 'Ossi' Rohr from the penalty spot and Franz Krumm scored the winning goals.

Football during the war

On 1 September 1939 the Second World War began with the attack on Poland by German armed forces. Almost every football player was called up for Hitler's army. Barely a club could field a complete team. And so it came about that the clubs were temporarily 'mixed' – and players from Bayern and 1860 Munich were despatched to the same eleven.

One of the 243 Bayern members who in 1939/40 had to put on a uniform was the defender Jakob Streitle.

The first Bayern champions' celebration with the old championship trophy, the Victoria.

zerland, as did the successful coach Dombi and prolific goalscorer 'Ossi' Rohr. So it was no wonder that FC Bayern was no longer very successful on the pitch. The best football in Germany was now being played in the Ruhr region: in Gelsenkirchen, by FC Schalke 04.

NO SUCCESS FOR BAYERN UNDER HITLER

After the seizure of power by the National Socialists under their 'Führer' Adolf Hitler on 30 January 1933, the whole of German sport was turned upside down. Jewish members were expelled from the clubs, and FC Bayern, whose development the Jewish citizens had significantly influenced, was affected particularly badly. The long-time president Kurt Landauer, who was Jewish, had to resign from his post and was detained in the concentration camp Dachau. He later fled to Swit-

The 1932 final: Bayern striker 'Ossi' Rohr opens the scoring.

BAYERN'S BEST
THE FIRST STARS

Alongside the reliable left back **Emil Kutterer**, **Josef Pöttinger** and **Ludwig Hofmann** in particular were among the big Bayern stars in the 1920s. Pöttinger, a true Munich boy from the Neuhausen district, was an exceptionally accurate and cunning striker. In the 1925/26 season, when FC Bayern won the Southern German Championship, he scored 57 goals. 'Wiggerl' Hofmann, a technically gifted left winger, used an unusual ploy: he wore a right shoe on his left foot to put more spin on the ball. Unfortunately Kutterer, Pöttinger and Hofmann, who all regularly played for the national team, had retired or left the club when Bayern won its first national championship.

> **For Chrissakes**
> In the 1930s 'Lutte' Goldbrunner was a national team regular (39 caps) and was considered one of the best centre halves in Europe. Hardly a centre forward had a chance against him – until the Italian Piola came along. 'He got past me a few times, for Chrissakes,' he fumed.

THE CHAMPIONSHIP TEAM OF 1932

The defence around the German internationals **Sigmund Haringer** and **Conrad Heidkamp** was among the best in Germany at this time. The captain, Heidkamp, remained an important player for FC Bayern until 1944. The midfield positions were filled with different types of players. On the right **Robert 'Pius' Breindl** was convincing with his indomitable fighting spirit, and on the left **Ernst Nagelschmitz** impressed with his outstanding technique. The pivotal player was centre half **Ludwig 'Lutte' Goldbrunner**, who was an exceptional ball winner and strong in the air. The cunning **Franz Krumm** and **Josef Bergmaier**, a

dribbler with a ferocious shot, formed the right wing, the left was marshalled by **Hans Schmid** and **Hans Welker**, who'd come up through the club's youth ranks. A particularly interesting man played up front: **Oskar 'Ossi' Rohr**. The centre forward, who came from VfR Mannheim in 1930, stayed on for only 16 months in Munich but scored over 30 goals during this time. Having won four caps, he left Germany in 1933 to earn a lot of money with Racing Strasbourg in the French League. In Germany he was simply considered a 'deserter' and 'gladiator who sold himself abroad' – and was never called up to the national team again.

Josef Pöttinger

Ludwig Goldbrunner, Hans Welker, Franz Krumm, Emil Kutterer,
Ernst Nagelschmitz, Wilhelm 'Schimmy' Simetsreiter, Ludwig Hofmann

Oskar Rohr

Championship line-up

In the 1920s and 1930s football teams used a very offensive formation. They played with only two defenders but five forwards (two wingers, two inside forwards, one centre forward). The most important man was the centre half who distributed the ball.

The team that won the final for the national championship on 12 June 1932:

Bergmaier Krumm Rohr Schmid Welker

Breindl Goldbrunner Nagelschmitz

Haringer Heidkamp

Lechler

Josef Bergmaier

17

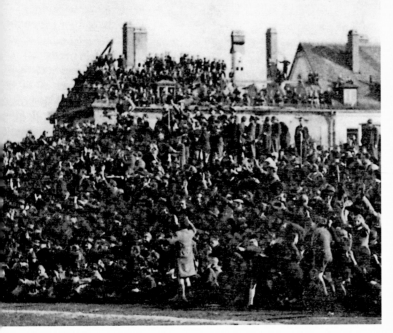

People watched the games at the Grünwalder Strasse ground even from demolished roofs in the neighbourhood.

THE OBERLIGA SOUTH AND THE FIRST CUP VICTORY

In the years after the war Bayern no longer enjoyed big successes. Prolific strikers had been Bayern's hallmark for decades, but now the attack wasn't scoring many goals anymore. On top of that, the defence had more holes than a Swiss cheese: in the 1949/50 season it conceded 70 goals! In the 1954/55 season the big catastrophe followed: Bayern finished last with only 15 points and was relegated to the second division of the southern tier. For the first time in the club's history, FC Bayern was a lower-league club!

The fans wanted the club to bounce back immediately and the players heeded the call. And some. Because only one year after being promoted again, Bayern completely unexpectedly won the DFB-Pokal for the first time. On 29 December 1957 they defeated the runaway favourite Fortuna Düsseldorf 1-0 in the Cup final. Unfortunately this was just a short-lived high. In the following years, the 'Red Shorts' only seldom found themselves among the top teams in the Oberliga South.

MATCHES IN THE DEMOLISHED STADIUM

During the war years from 1939 to 1945 matches could only continue with effort and hardship. After the Grünwalder Strasse ground had been destroyed by an aerial assault, Bayern had to move into the Dante Stadium. Despite the sombre conditions, they managed to win the championship of the district (then called a 'Gau') of Southern Bavaria in 1944. When the new Oberliga South was created after the war (one of the five regional divisions that made up the top level of the German game), they moved back to Grünwalder Strasse – even though the stadium was still clearly scarred by traces of the destruction.

Oberliga football in the post-war years: FC Bayern against BC Augsburg

The 1957 DFB-Pokal winners.

In the Bundesliga promotion play-offs, FC Bayern promptly won the first match against Tennis Borussia Berlin 2-0.

PROMOTION TO THE BUNDESLIGA

When the Bundesliga was formed in 1963, Bayern was not a part of it. Only the clubs that had achieved the best results in the previous years were allowed to play in the Bundesliga. And from the Oberliga South that meant FC Nuremberg, Eintracht Frankfurt, VfB Stuttgart, Karlsruher SC and 1860 Munich. FC Bayern had to stay in the second division (then called 'Regionalliga'). Under the new coach 'Čik' Cajkovski, who had built the team around young talent, Bayern took the Regionalliga by storm in 1964/65: 146 league goals (in 36 matches) constitute an all-time record! The 19-year-old centre forward Gerd Müller alone scored 33 goals. In the promotional play-offs that followed, against Tennis Borussia Berlin, FC Saarbrücken and Alemannia Aachen, the 'Red Shorts' prevailed just as effortlessly scoring 18 goals and conceding only 3. Bayern's big success could now begin.

Every Bayern player received a hat as a gift for being promoted to the Oberliga in 1956.

BAYERN'S BEST
THE OBERLIGA STARS

The trusted defender and centre half **Jakob Streitle** broke into Bayern's first team as early as 1935 and remained one of the team leaders for many years after the war. **Herbert Moll**, a tall midfielder, was in the 1940s said to be a model of dedication and fairness. **Gerhard Siedl**, a cunning goalscorer, was among the best forwards in German football in the 1950s. The left back **Hans Bauer** was the record player of FC Bayern in the Oberliga South between 1948 and 1959 (226 appearances) and the captain of the 1957 DFB-Pokal winners. Bauer made two appearances at the 1954 World Cup. The midfielder **Karl Mai**, who joined FC Bayern from SpVgg Fürth in 1958, really can call himself a World Cup winner: he was on the pitch when (West) Germany won the final 3-2 against Hungary. **Adolf Kunstwadl** was a mainstay in Bayern's defence between 1961 and 1965.

The left winger **Dieter 'Mucki' Brenninger** was also a danger to be reckoned with: he alone scored 24 goals in the 1963/64 Regionalliga season. After the promotion to the Bundesliga in 1965, he remained a dangerous man with a fantastic scoring record. **Werner Olk**, defender and captain in the years 1965 to 1970, was christened 'the Eagle from Giesing' due to his acrobatic stunts in his own penalty area. **Peter Kupferschmidt** was often nervous and was hence named 'Psycho' by his team-mates; rarely did an opponent get past the defender, however. The good-looking tricky dribbler **Rudolf Nafziger** was one of the first Bayern players to bring the girls swarming in. **Rainer Ohlhauser** turned out to be an unbelievably consistent striker in the Oberliga and Regionalliga days. He scored 42 goals alone in the 1964/65 promotion season (in 36 matches!).

Brenninger, Olk, Kupferschmidt, Nafziger and Ohlhauser were also in the team that won the 1967 Cup Winners' Cup – together with three young players with whom every German fan is still familiar today: Sepp Maier, Franz Beckenbauer and Gerd Müller.

The veteran Jakob Streitle hands over the ball to a young Hans Bauer. Cover page of Der Kicker *from January 1952. In those days Bayern was famous for having great defenders.*

Autograph cards of the Oberliga stars (from top): Rudolf Nafziger,
Werner Olk, Peter Kupferschmidt, Dieter Brenninger, Rainer
Ohlhauser, Adolf Kunstwadl
Main picture, middle: Herbert Moll

THE GOLDEN AGE

FC Bayern 1966–1976

League champions 1969, 1972, 1973, 1974

DFB-Pokal winners 1966, 1967, 1969, 1971

European Cup winners 1974, 1975, 1976

Winners of the Cup Winners' Cup 1967

Intercontinental Cup winner 1976

The Bayern team before the Cup Winners' Cup final in 1967 (1-0 against Rangers).

1967: TRIUMPH IN THE CUP WINNERS' CUP

In 1965/66, their first Bundesliga season, the young Bayern team, in which Franz Beckenbauer meanwhile held down a regular place alongside goalkeeper Sepp Maier and target man Gerd Müller, played well from the off. They scored 71 goals and finished the season in 3rd place. The team was even more successful in the Cup competition. Dortmund, Braunschweig, Cologne, Hamburg and Nuremberg were all defeated. In the final they won 4-2 after extra time against MSV Duisburg in front of a crowd of 60,000 at the Waldstadion in Frankfurt. In doing so Bayern qualified for the Cup Winners' Cup. And they actually lifted this trophy, too: after they had eliminated Tatran Prešov, Shamrock Rovers, Rapid Vienna and Standard Liège, Rangers awaited them in the final. In front of 70,000 spectators in Nuremberg it was still scoreless after 90 minutes. The game went to extra time and in the 108th minute, Franz 'The Bull' Roth scored the goal that won it for FC Bayern.

After winning the Cup Winners' Cup, coach Cajkovski was lifted up by the players.

Top: Gerd Müller, Dieter Brenninger and 'Katsche' Schwarzenbeck celebrate the DFB-Pokal victory in 1969.
Right: Under Cajkovski, Bayern improved their skills, for instance by having to put the ball into baskets instead of goals.

ADDITIONAL CUPS

For Bayern, the first title in Europe was not enough. Just a few days after the victory against Rangers, they were in the DFB-Pokal final again. This time their opponent was Hamburger SV, the result 4-0. The team led by Maier, Beckenbauer and Müller would not win the Cup Winners' Cup again, but it remained successful in the domestic cup competition. Bayern won the 1969 final 2-1 against Schalke and followed that with a 2-1 victory over FC Cologne in the 1971 final. Within six years, Bayern had won the German Cup four times!

THE FIRST SUCCESSFUL COACHES

Bayern's style underwent a striking transformation within a few years. Under 'Čik' Cajkovski, a man who was always in good spirits and coached Bayern until 1968, the team played a ferocious, offensive game. The motto: 'Win in great style or go down'. His grouchy successor Branko Zebec, coach until 1970, focussed on discipline and a more cautious approach. Now the motto was 'It's not beauty that counts, but above all victory'. Now the team was also playing more consistently in the Bundesliga. It was certainly no coincidence that FC Bayern won their first league title once Zebec had arrived, namely in the 1968/69 season. Previously, Bayern had often won by many goals but also suffered some heavy defeats.

The team that won the Cup Winners' Cup final in 1967

Bayern's formation in the Cup Winners' Cup final on 31 May 1967:

Nafziger Ohlhauser Müller Brenninger

Roth Koulmann

Nowak Beckenbauer Olk Kupferschmidt

Maier

The opponents in the final: Rangers from Scotland

Footballing wisdoms
Gerd Müller: 'If you start thinking, it's too late anyway.'
Sepp Maier: 'A goalkeeper must exude calm. But he has to watch out that he doesn't fall asleep doing it.'
Franz Beckenbauer: 'You can win every match, but you can also lose every match.'

REPEAT CHAMPIONS IN THE BUNDESLIGA

In the 1967/68 season Bayern had scored 68 goals, but had also let in 58. They couldn't do better than 5th place. In 1968/69, in the first season under Branko Zebec, Bayern scored 62 goals and conceded only 31. In the end, Bayern took its first Bundesliga title by a big margin over runners-up Alemannia Aachen! The key player was Gerd Müller, who scored 30 goals. In the following years the dominant team was Borussia Mönchengladbach (German champions 1970 and 1971). Finally, under Udo Lattek, Bayern moved over to the fast lane. The new coach bolstered the team with ambitious up-and-coming players, such as Paul Breitner and Uli Hoeness. And he managed to humour the

The father of Bayern's success: coach Udo Lattek.

established Bayern players, who were now celebrated stars. The team delivered and was almost always successful, both in the league and in the cup. Three times in a row – 1972, 1973 and 1974 – Lattek and his team won the Bundesliga title. In 1971/72, Bayern set a record that still stands by scoring 101 goals. Gerd Müller alone netted 40 (in 34 games)!

League champion 1973: Sepp Maier leads the lap of honour in the Olympic Stadium.

Bayern and the 'Foals'

Between 1968/69 and 1976/77, only two clubs won the Bundesliga: Bayern Munich and Borussia Mönchengladbach. Because of their youth, the players from Mönchengladbach were nicknamed the 'Foals' and were even more successful than FC Bayern: while Bayern won four league titles, Borussia managed five. Legend has it that the 'Foals', led by Günter Netzer, played better, more offensive football than the 'Red Shorts' from Munich. But this cannot be completely correct: during those nine years, Bayern won only one title less, but scored a total of 715 goals – Gladbach, meanwhile, scored 'only' 676. It is true, however, that the 'Foals' were less successful on the European stage. They won only two UEFA Cups (now the Europa League). Bayern on the other hand was able to top off their success in the Bundesliga with triumphs in the European Cup.

Record transfer
After Bayern had reached the peak of German football in 1972, they could now afford to sign expensive stars for the first time: ahead of the 1973/74 season, Jupp Kapellmann from FC Cologne joined for the record transfer fee of 800,000 German marks (at the time, this equalled £125,000).

The captains and playmakers of the two best teams of the 1970s: Franz Beckenbauer and Günter Netzer.

1974: THE FIRST TRIUMPH IN THE EUROPEAN CUP

At the beginning of the 1970s, Ajax Amsterdam was the best team in Europe. The footballers from the capital of the Netherlands had won the European Cup three times in a row from 1971 to 1973. Bayern, meanwhile, didn't have much success in this competition, a 4-0 home defeat at the hands of Ajax on 7 March 1973 was particularly painful. In the same year, however, Bayern mounted a new challenge to the European elite – and this time with success. They were able to defeat Åtvidabergs FF, Dynamo Dresden, ZSKA Sofia and Újpest Budapest. On 15 May 1974 the final was staged at the Heysel Stadium in Brussels; the opponents were Atlético Madrid.

The Spaniards had an unexpectedly great game, especially in the second half. Only with luck and thanks to the class of Beckenbauer and Maier could Bayern manage to keep the game scoreless until extra time. When Atlético's midfielder Luis Aragonés curled a free kick past Sepp Maier into the net after 114 minutes, the game appeared to be over. But then came the 120th minute, the last minute of extra time: Georg Schwarzenbeck intercepted a

Opponents in the final: Atlético Madrid from Spain.

pass, couldn't find an unmarked teammate and simply took a shot from some 30 yards – and made it 1-1. It was the first ever European goal by the rugged centre half.

Because final matches were not decided with penalty shoot-outs in those days, both teams had to meet just two days later, again in Brussels, for a rematch. This time Bayern was stronger. Atlético's team, in which there were many older players, couldn't cope physically. Striker Gerd Müller and the lightning-fast Uli Hoeness were the best men on the pitch and scored two goals each. It was a terrific victory and the 4-0 scoreline was thoroughly deserved.

FC Bayern wins the European Cup for the first time.

The team that won the European Cup final on 17 May 1974

Torstensson   Müller   Hoeneß

Kapellmann   Zobel   Roth

Beckenbauer

Breitner   Schwarzenbeck   Hansen

Maier

SPYING ON BAYERN

At the beginning of the 1970s the so-called Cold War was fought between the Western powers under the leadership of the USA and the Eastern Bloc under the leadership of what was then called the Soviet Union. The border between these two groups ran through the middle of Germany, which was split into West Germany (FRG) and East Germany (GDR). That is why Bayern were nervous when they had to travel to the GDR to meet Dynamo Dresden. There were rumours that West German players could be spied upon or even poisoned. Bayern's president Wilhelm Neudecker therefore decided not to let his team stay overnight in the East German Hotel Newa in Dresden, which had already been hired out, but in the West German town Hof, close to the border. The 3,000 East German fans who froze for hours outside the hotel in order to greet the famous Bayern players were disappointed beyond measure.

The decision by Neudecker was exaggerated, but not entirely unfounded. Nobody wanted to poison Bayern, but they were being monitored by the GDR state security, whose technicians had equipped the hotel's salon with concealed microphones. While Bayern did not spend the night at this hotel, coach Udo Lattek held his pre-match team talk there. The spies jotted down the line-up and gave it to Walter Fritsch, the Dresden coach. Thus Dynamo was well-informed about Bayern's formation and tactics before the game even began. But it was not of much use. Early into the match Uli Hoeness twice left his marker Eduard Geyer in his wake and gave Bayern a 2-0 lead. The game finished 3-3, but since Bayern had won the first leg 4-3, they were through to the next round.

With this odd explanation, president Neudecker justified his decision to let the Bayern team stay in Hof and not in Dresden: 'The difference in altitude between Munich and Dresden could inhibit our performance, and maybe two days is not enough to acclimatise to it.'

The 1973/74 European Cup round of 16: Bayern draws 3-3 in Dresden.

CRISIS FOR BAYERN IN THE BUNDESLIGA

Only a few weeks after the European Cup triumph, six Bayern players (Maier, Beckenbauer, Schwarzenbeck, Breitner, Hoeness and Müller), who had already won the 1972 European Championships, earned the right to also call themselves World Cup winners. Breitner and Müller were on target as (West) Germany won the World Cup final 2-1 against a strong Dutch team. Bayern's best players had now won everything you can win as a footballer. It was rather understandable that their performances dropped off in the next Bundesliga season. The inevitable happened: Bayern changed the coach. In January 1975 Udo Lattek was replaced by Dettmar Cramer. When Cramer took over, Bayern were in 14th place – a terrible showing for this proud club. The coach couldn't quite get the team back to its winning ways and Bayern finished the season in 10th place. In the two seasons that followed, Bayern again did not make it to the top. But there was still the European Cup!

The opponent in the 1975 and 1976 finals: Leeds United from England and St. Etienne from France.

THE EUROPEAN CUP VICTORIES OF 1975 AND 1976

While Bayern, now with future superstar Karl-Heinz Rummenigge, were mired in mid-table in the Bundesliga, they continued to have success in Europe. In the 1974/75 European Cup, they eliminated FC Magdeburg, Ararat Yerevan and St. Etienne before meeting Leeds United in the final in Paris on 28 May 1975. It was one of the ugliest games in the history of the European Cup. The English team committed one foul after the other. Uli Hoeness's knee was so badly injured that in later years he never quite got back his former strength. In the end, a patient Bayern team defeated Leeds 2-0 with goals from Franz 'The Bull' Roth and Gerd Müller. Bayern had defended the trophy and earned the right to compete in the following season's European Cup as title-holders, even though they were still a mid-table club in the Bundesliga. The opponents in the 1975/76 competition were Jeunesse Esch, Malmö FF

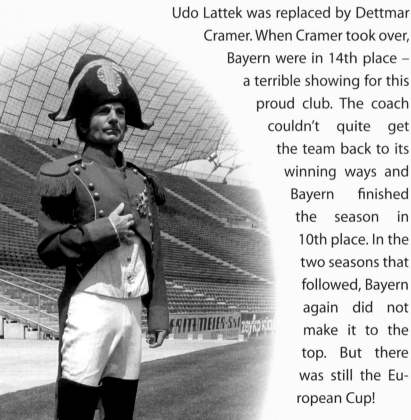

After the diminutive Dettmar Cramer had lifted the European Cup twice, he allowed himself to be photographed as Napoleon.

Celebrating after the final against Leeds.

Maier and Hansen after the third European Cup victory in 1976.

and Benfica as well as Real Madrid in the semi-final. While the German champions Borussia Mönchengladbach had been knocked out by Real in the quarter-finals, Bayern went through with a 2-0 win at home after drawing 1-1 in the first leg. The final was won by the narrowest of margins against St. Etienne from France – once again Franz 'The Bull' Roth scored the only goal of the night. Even though they did not always play well in the Bundesliga and their victories in the European Cup were narrow and not always great to watch, Bayern could call themselves the best team on the continent, having won three European Cups in a row.

END OF THE GLORY DAYS

Several results from the 1976/77 Bundesliga season tell you that the mighty Bayern team was on the decline. On the sixth matchday, Bayern were trailing 4-0 in Bochum. However, they still had enough class to fight back and avoid defeat, scoring five goals in 20 minutes! Final score: 6-5 to Bayern. But then some bad losses followed. Matchday 9: Bayern Munich vs Schalke 04 0-7. Matchday 28: Hamburger SV vs Bayern Munich 5-0.

Matchday 30: FC Saarbrücken vs Bayern Munich 6-1. Despite such heavy defeats, Bayern finished the season in 7th place. But the team was falling apart. At the end of the season Franz Beckenbauer bid farewell and went to the United States. Without their outstanding captain the team were losing even more frequently. During the 1977/78 season, after six defeats in a row, coach Dettmar Cramer had to leave. His successor Gyula Lorant managed to avoid relegation, but of course no-one at Bayern was happy with a 12th-place finish.

Intercontinental Cup
The Intercontinental Cup pitted the best clubs from Europe and South America against each other and wasn't considered that big a title. Still, Bayern were happy to win it for the first time in 1976 over two legs (2-0, 0-0) against the Brazilian club Belo Horizonte.

Franz Beckenbauer played his last game for Bayern in 1977.

BAYERN'S BEST
THE STARS OF THE 1970s (1)

Sweeper

In the old days, the last man at the back was called the 'stopper'. He never left his defensive position and would clear dangerous situations by simply hoofing the ball upfield. Franz Beckenbauer reinvented this role by becoming the 'free man', or modern sweeper (the Italian word is 'libero'). Beckenbauer not only organised the defence but also built from the rear and initiated attacks.

The three world-class players Maier, Beckenbauer and Müller (the goalkeeper, the sweeper and the centre forward, respectively) formed the heart of the Bayern team that dominated European football in the mid-1970s. **Franz Beckenbauer** joined Bayern as a 13-year-old in 1964. At first the youngster from Giesing (a working-class district of Munich) was a forward, but gradually he was used in a more defensive role. In his twelve years with FC Bayern, Beckenbauer lifted every trophy a footballer can win. Due to his exceptional ball skills he always looked elegant and gave the impression of never having to put in an effort on the pitch. This earned him the reverential nickname 'Kaiser' (emperor). However, some fans preferred to see players sweat and toil and they criticised him for his casual style that sometimes appeared arrogant. His success, though, spoke for itself. Beckenbauer was the first German footballer to win more than 100 caps. In May 1977, he moved to Cosmos New York for a large sum of money, where he played with the legendary Brazilian Pelé and other stars. In 1980 he had a short comeback in the Bundesliga with Hamburg. After he hung up his boots, he was also successful as a coach with the national team (winning the 1990 World Cup), Olympique Marseille and FC Bayern. Beckenbauer (who was also Bayern's president from 1994 to 2009) is more famous throughout the world than any other German and is considered one of the best footballers of all time.

Sepp Maier, who joined Bayern from small TSV Haar, originally wanted to be an actor, but starting in 1962 would make Bayern's goal his stage. Maier was seen as a very lithe goalkeeper and was known as 'the Cat from Anzing', after his hometown. The goalkeeper, who would often indulge in a meatloaf roll at the stadium kiosk half an hour before kick-off, not only made fantastic saves but also loved to play the clown and make jokes. He kept Bayern's goal for 17 years and went to four World Cups with (West) Germany. His dream of a fifth World Cup died on 14 July 1979 when he suffered a serious car accident that would end

Franz Beckenbauer in 1972

certainly never be bettered, as the man they called the 'Nation's Bomber' scored 68 goals in only 62 internationals! He finished his career in the United States with the Fort Lauderdale Strikers. Since 1992, Germany's greatest-ever striker has been working with Bayern's reserves and youth teams.

Sepp Maier pursued not only balls and ducks but occasionally also toy balloons.

Ducks
Sometimes Sepp Maier wouldn't try to catch balls but rather pursued other flying objects, such as toy balloons or ducks. In May 1976, a duck waddled across Bayern's penalty box during a Bundesliga match against VfL Bochum. Sepp Maier stalked up on it, dived acrobatically – but the duck was not to be caught.

his career. Maier opened a tennis centre in Anzing and also became goalkeeper coach for both the national team and FC Bayern.

When the legendary poacher **Gerd Müller** joined Bayern from his local club TSV Nördlingen in 1964, coach 'Čik' Cajkovski was not enthusiastic. 'What am I supposed to do with a weightlifter?' he asked. But he then recognised the qualities of the player he liked to call 'the small fat one'. Müller scored 32 goals in 26 matches as Bayern won promotion in 1964/65. Then, in the Bundesliga, he would win the Golden Boot seven times until he left Germany during the 1977/78 season. Müller was so lethal in front of goal that the journalists coined a new word for his style of goalscoring, they called it 'to müller'. He made 585 appearances for FC Bayern in competitive games, scoring 533 goals. His record for (West) Germany will

Gerd Müller in action.

33

BAYERN'S BEST
THE STARS OF THE 1970s (2)

Uli Hoeness

Franz Roth, a farmer's son from the Allgäu region, was very strong and so his team-mates called him the 'Bull'. Whenever the powerful Roth, who liked to scoff down a roast or a strawberry tart before a game, ran towards his opponents, they could barely stop him. For twelve years Roth played in the Bayern midfield and was a huge goalscoring threat, particularly on the European stage. He scored the deciding goal in the 1967 Cup Winners' Cup final against Rangers and also in the European Cup finals of 1975 (against Leeds) and 1976 (St. Etienne). Roth had to end his career in 1977 after twice tearing his Achilles tendon.

The brawny centre half **Georg 'Katsche' Schwarzenbeck** gained fame as Franz Beckenbauer's 'deputy'. Whenever the sweeper moved forward, the always reliable 'Katsche' covered his back. The centre half, who usually looked rather awkward, did not garner many plaudits for it: journalists joked that he was simply 'Franz's third foot'. Yet to his opponents, who called him 'Frankenstein' because of his hard way of playing, he was fearsome. Schwarzenbeck proved just how valuable he was not only in club football, but also on the international stage. (West) Germany lost only five out of the 44 games he played for his country. In 1980, 'Katsche' was forced to finish his career due to a torn Achilles tendon. In his second career, he ran a small store in Munich that supplied the FC Bayern offices with stationery.

Georg Schwarzenbeck

Franz Roth

In 1970, he joined FC Bayern together with Paul Breitner and coach Udo Lattek. Soon everybody was talking about him. Not only because he scored great goals but also because he always had a snappy, outspoken quip at the ready. Hoeness's career, during which he also earned quite a lot of money through non-footballing activities and businesses, was cut short very early due to a knee injury. After a final comeback attempt with FC Nuremberg in 1978/79, he had to give up football at 27 years of age. Even before that season was over, he started his second career as FC Bayern's business manager – and would become so famous in this role that people almost forgot he had been a great footballer.

There were other men who played a role in the big triumphs of the 1970s, who today are not so well known: there were the Dane Johnny Hansen and the inconspicuous Udo Horsman at the back, the hard-working Rainer Zobel, Bernd Dürnberger and Jupp Kapellmann in midfield, and the Swede Conny Torstensson upfront.

During his first stint at Bayern (1970–74), left back **Paul Breitner** not only caught people's attention with his footballing skills but also with his afro hairdo and his critical and controversial statements. In 1974, the rebel and stickler went to Real Madrid for a fee of 2m German Marks (at the time, that equalled £330,000), where he won one Spanish Cup and two league titles. After his return to the Bundesliga in 1977, he spent one season in Braunschweig before embarking on a second Bayern career as the side's playmaker. Until 1983 he remained the undisputed team leader. After his active career, he coached youth teams, wrote newspaper columns and worked as a pundit for television. Since 2007, he's back at FC Bayern as an adviser.

Uli Hoeness, the son of a butcher from Ulm, caught people's eyes at a young age due to his fast solo runs.

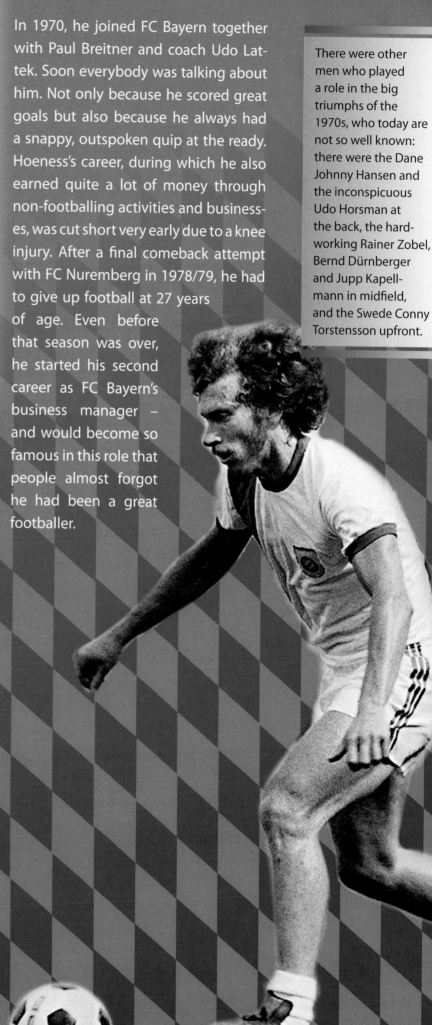

Paul Breitner

CRISES, CHAOS AND TRIUMPHS

FC Bayern in the 1980s and 1990s

Bundesliga champions 1980, 1981, 1985, 1986, 1987, 1989, 1990, 1994, 1997, 1999

DFB-Pokal winners 1982, 1984, 1986, 1998

UEFA Cup winners 1996

European Cup/Champions League finalists 1982, 1987, 1999

THE BAYERN REVOLUTION

During the 1978/79 season there was an event that is unique in German football history: the players staged a 'revolt' against the club's management. Uli Hoeness had already joined FC Nuremberg to get away from the stern coach Gyula Lorant when the latter was ripe for dismissal after a 7-1 defeat in Düsseldorf. Bayern president Wilhelm Neudecker wanted to replace him with Max Merkel, feared as a slave-driver. But the players, led by captain Sepp Maier and Paul Breitner (who had just returned to Munich), preferred assistant coach Pal Csernai. When the president realised he could not get his own way, he resigned. Csernai was made the new head coach.

'BREITNIGGE' AND CONSTANT SUCCESS

Former player Uli Hoeness now held the reins as the club's business manager, while Paul Breitner, the last of the 'old' Bayern guard, was in charge on the pitch. Breitner orchestrated play from the back and the young striker Karl-Heinz Rummenigge took care of scoring goals upfront. The two linked up so well that they were soon considered an inseparable duo and dubbed 'Breitnigge'. And so, as 'FC Breitnigge', Bayern was soon bringing silverware to Munich: they won the league two years running, 1980 and 1981, and the German Cup, the DFB-Pokal, in 1982. During the 1983/84 season, coach Udo Lattek returned to replace Pal Csernai. Over the next few

Top: The stern coach Max Merkel.
Right: Rummenigge and Breitner alias 'Breitnigge'.

1981: The champions celebrate (left: Karl-Heinz Rummenigge).

Constant Rivals
Werder Bremen

In the 1980s, Werder Bremen took over from Borussia Mönchengladbach as Bayern's closest rivals. The 1985/86 season was particularly memorable. In the first half of the season, a harsh foul from Bayern defender Klaus Augenthaler on Werder forward Rudi Völler during Bremen's 3-1 defeat in Munich led to bad feelings between the two clubs. When the teams met in Bremen for the return match, on the penultimate day of the season, Bremen held a two-point lead over Bayern in the league, which meant that a win would have won them the Bundesliga. But the game ended scoreless, because Bremen's Kutzop missed a penalty in the 89th minute, hitting the post! On the final matchday, FC Bayern won 6-0 against Mönchengladbach, while Werder were beaten 2-1 in Stuttgart. The teams were level on points, but Bayern won the league thanks to their superior goal difference.

years, Bayern reaped more successes as if by default: Bundesliga titles in 1985, 1986 and 1987 and the DFB-Pokal in 1984 and 1986. Finally, Breitner finished his career and Rummenigge moved to Internazionale (Inter Milan) in 1984 for the then-record sum of 11.4m German Marks (at the time, that was £3m). Now players such as Klaus Augenthaler, Soren Lerby, Lothar Matthäus and Uli Hoeness's brother Dieter were setting the tone. Eight domestic titles in the 1980s (six in the league and two in the cup) – not a bad tally.

Turban
In the 13th minute of the 1982 German Cup final against FC Nuremberg, Dieter Hoeness sustained a bloody head injury from a collision with his marker Reinhardt. Hoeness played the rest of the game with a head bandage, nicknamed a 'turban'. In the 89th minute, he headed home (!) to put the finishing touch on Bayern's 4-2 win.

Bremen's player Kutzop misses the deciding penalty against Bayern.

DREAMING OF A NEW REAL MADRID

As Uli Hoeness took over as Bayern's business manager in 1979, he had a big dream: he wanted to make 'his' Bayern the new Real Madrid. The Spanish giants were regarded as the best, most distinguished and richest club in Europe. Between 1956 and 1960, Real, who always played entirely in white, had won the European Cup five times in a row. No club had been quite as dominating since. Bayern, Hoeness felt, should be just as successful and the football fans should rave about Bayern as they once did about Real. But success in the European Cup was not as easy to come by as it was in the Bundesliga.

DEFEATED BY ASTON VILLA

Bayern's first chance in this decade to win the most coveted trophy in Europe came on 26 May 1982. The team met English league winners Aston Villa in the European Cup final in Rotterdam (Holland). En route to this final, FC Bayern had eliminated, among others, the reigning champions from Romania and Bulgaria. Villa didn't field a team the Germans had to fear, but it was perhaps precisely for this reason that Bayern underestimated their opponents. The overwhelming favourites from Munich, with Klaus Augenthaler, Paul Breitner, Dieter Hoeness and Karl-Heinz Rummenigge, enjoyed more ball possession and had many chances. But it was the team from Birmingham that scored the only goal of the night from a counter-attack on 67 minutes to decide the game.

Left: Real Madrid's wonder team that won the European Cup five times in a row (1956–60) was Bayern's role model. Right: Dieter Hoeness (at the back) and Paul Breitner can hardly believe their bad luck after the 1-0 defeat against Aston Villa in 1982.

Losing Against Porto

Five years later, Bayern celebrated a phenomenal victory over their role models Real Madrid in the European Cup semi-final. In a rough game in Mu-

When 'Wiggerl' Kögl scored against Porto in the final, Bayern appeared to be cruising

nich's Olympic Stadium, Bayern were the better team and won 4-1. The team then survived Real's onslaught in the second leg and only lost 1-0 in front of 103,000 spectators in Madrid – what could go wrong now? On 27 May 1987 the final was staged in Vienna (Austria), the opponents were FC Porto from Portugal. In the days leading up to the game, the mood among Bayern's players and fans was excellent. They had beaten mighty Real – so the champions from Portugal should not pose a big problem. Everything seemed to go according to plan. The young, nippy winger Ludwig 'Wiggerl' Kögl, who only rarely found the target, gave Bayern the lead in the 25th minute. There was no further score until deep into the second half. Then came the 78th minute. Bayern's Hans Pflügler deflected a cross and the ball spun behind the back of Porto's Algerian forward Rabah Madjer through the penalty box. Madjer coolly back-heeled it into the net. The entire Bayern team, including midfield maestro Lothar Matthäus, was under shock and lost control of the game. Porto went on to score another goal and won the match 2-1.

1987, after the 2-1 at the hands of Porto: Norbert Nachtweih, Lothar Matthäus, Norbert Eder and Michael Rummenigge are shocked.

BAYERN'S BEST
THE STARS
OF THE 1980s

On 21 August 1982, the Belgian **Jean-Marie Pfaff**, who came from a family of artists, had a terrible start in the Bayern goal. In the game against Werder Bremen he went up to catch a throw-in from Uwe Reinders – but the ball skimmed the tips of his fingers and landed in the goal. He could, in fact, have let the ball pass, because according to the rules a direct goal from a throw-in does not count. Despite this misfortune, Pfaff was a world-class goalkeeper and became a regular starter. Later he was followed by **Raimond Aumann** from Augsburg after a fierce duel for the number-one shirt. Like his predecessor, Aumann, who was known as Baloo after the *Jungle Book* bear, was much loved by the fans. Perhaps because of this he later became Bayern's supporter liaison officer. **Klaus Augenthaler**,

Klaus Augenthaler

from Fürstenzell in Lower Bavaria, was Beckenbauer's successor. He was feared by all opponents for his fighting spirit and shooting power. As a Bavarian through and through, he became Bayern's undisputed team leader after the departure of Paul Breitner. This 1990 World Cup winner marshalled the defence and held the team together for 15 years. After the end of his active career, 'Auge' was initially made assistant coach at FC Bayern and later became the head coach for a number of different clubs in the Bundesliga.

Hans Pflügler from Freising, just north of Munich, who today is in charge of the club's merchandise department, proved to be a consistently reliable defender from 1981 onwards. Another mainstay in the Bayern back line was **Norbert Nachtweih**, who had fled from the GDR.

In 1983, business manager Uli Hoeness succeeded in signing a midfield star from Ajax Amsterdam who was in great demand – **Soren Lerby**. Over three seasons, the creative Dane proved to be a fierce competitor. Off the pitch, though, he was always in good spirits. From October 1991 to March 1992 Lerby dabbled at being Bayern's head coach, but this position demanded too much of him.

The transfer of **Karl-Heinz Rummenigge**, who joined from Borussia Lippstadt in 1974 and later went on to become a world-class forward, cost Bayern a total of just 17,500 German Marks (less than £3,000 at the time). At first he was very shy (and nicknamed Ruddy Cheeks) and did not score that of ten. He finally broke through in his sixth year in the Bundesliga (1979/80) when he scored 26 goals. That 'Kalle', as he was called, suddenly found the net was the result of a special training regimen. In 1984, as a three-time Bundesliga Golden Boot winner, he moved to Internazionale for the then record transfer fee of 11.4m German Marks. In 1991, Rummenigge was elected vice-president of FC Bayern, since 2002 he is the club's chairman.

For his brother Uli, **Dieter Hoeness** was the best buy of his managerial ca-

Jean-Marie Pfaff

reer. The younger of the Hoeness brothers joined from VfB Stuttgart in 1979 for only 175,000 German Marks (about £44,000 back then). The 'lanky one' always appeared stiff and immobile but turned out to be an efficient and dangerous centre forward for eight years (102 goals). Later he became business manager of VfB Stuttgart, Hertha BSC and VfL Wolfsburg. Even more successful for FC Bayern was **Roland Wohlfarth**, who had joined from MSV Duisburg in 1984. He played in Munich for nine years and during that time scored 119 goals. Oddly enough, however, he never became a real star. The diminutive **Ludwig 'Wiggerl' Kögl**, who stood 5 feet 7 inches, came to Bayern in 1984 from local rivals 1860. The winger never became much of a goalscoring threat but was loved by the fans for his mazy runs and dribblings.

Dieter Hoeness

Raimond Aumann

Norbert Nachtweih

Soren Lerby

Roland Wohlfarth

Hans Pflügler

Ludwig Kögl

Karl-Heinz Rummenigge

The 1990 champions take a bath – but coach Heynckes will soon be in deep waters.

In the 1996 UEFA Cup finals, Bayern beat Girondins Bordeaux from France.

THE BIG CRISIS

Jupp Heynckes, who took over from Udo Lattek as coach in 1987, did not just want success for Bayern but also exciting, attacking football. In order to improve the team, several strikers from abroad were now being signed. Players such as Mark Hughes (Wales), Johnny Ekström (Sweden), Radmilo Mihajlovic (from the former Yugoslavia), Alan McInally (Scotland) and Mazinho (Brazil). However, they did not live up to their promise. More precisely, they were scoring not enough goals. Thanks to the tried-and-trusted team leader Klaus Augenthaler, Heynckes did guide the team to the league championships in 1989 and 1990, but the rot set in soon after 'Auge' had retired. In 1991/92 FC Bayern, now lacking players with leadership qualities, sank like a stone down the table. Heynckes could no longer wield authority and was sacked; his successor Lerby quit after a few weeks. Finally, Erich Ribbeck took over and led the team to a 10th-place finish.

THE 'KAISER' AND THE 'LOSERS' CUP'

The following years were rarely quiet in Munich. Coaches changed frequently. Whether Erich Ribbeck, Giovanni Trapattoni or Otto Rehhagel – they were all constantly criticised. Franz Beckenbauer twice took over the managerial hot seat himself (replacing Ribbeck in 1994 and Rehhagel in 1996), and both times he was successful: in 1994 he won the league and in 1996 the UEFA Cup. In the two-legged final, Bayern beat the French team Girondins Bordeaux 2-0 and 3-1. It was the first European title in 20 years, but the 'Kaiser' was not satisfied. He would have preferred to have won the Champions League, as the European Cup was now called. The UEFA Cup, he said disparagingly, was just the 'Losers' Cup'.

Otto Rehhagel conducts a training session by megaphone. It was loud – but the players still didn't always listen to him.

'FC Hollywood'

In the 1990s, the press coined the name 'FC Hollywood' for FC Bayern. What they meant was that the show had become more important than the game in Munich. Footballers were now treated like pop stars. The newspaper and television journalists, meanwhile, were always looking for sensational stories, and many players were only too willing to comply by carrying out their conflicts in public. Things were particularly bad between Lothar Matthäus and Jürgen Klinsmann, who did not get along at all and complained about each other. Add to this that Franz Beckenbauer, president since 1994, regularly changed his mind about all kinds of things, which led to confusion. But despite the turmoil, Bayern remained successful. During his second stint with Bayern (1996–98), the Italian Giovanni Trapattoni lifted a league title and the German cup, the DFB-Pokal.

Playmaker Lothar Matthäus caused the greatest unrest at Bayern. He often spoke when he would have done better to keep silent.

eadlines from the 1990s

ugust 1990, DFB-Pokal: Bayern are beaten 1-0 at amateur b FV 09 Weinheim.

April 1994, Bundesliga: Thomas Helmer scored a goal ainst FC Nuremberg that wasn't a goal at all (the ball had t crossed the line, as the referee thought, but had rolled into uch just outside the left-hand post). Because of this 'phan- m goal', the game had to be replayed (Bayern won this one -0).

4 August 1994, DFB-Pokal: Bayern lose 1-0 at amateur club 'SV Vestenbergsgreuth.

15 April 1995, Bundesliga: Bayern win 5-2 against Eintracht Frankfurt, but the game is annulled and the points awarded to Frankfurt, because coach Trapattoni has broken the rules by fielding four 'amateurs' (players not signed to a professional contract).

18 May 1996, Bundesliga: During the season finale against Fortuna Düsseldorf (2-2), Bayern coach Klaus Augenthaler inadvertently substitutes four (!) players at half-time. Only three substitutions are allowed. Düsseldorf don't file a protest, though, because nothing is at stake anymore.

10 May 1997, Bundesliga: Having been taken off for an unknown player called Lakies after 80 minutes of the game against last-placed SC Freiburg, Jürgen Klinsmann snapped. He verbally abused Giovanni Trapattoni and angrily kicked an advertising display.

Jürgen Klinsmann's furious kick.

ROTATION POLICY

Given the huge number of games in the Bundesliga, the domestic cup and the Champions League, Ottmar Hitzfeld introduced a rotation policy. It meant that all players, even the best, were benched at regular intervals in order to be given a rest. The coach managed to explain to his players that this was a sensible measure and not 'punishment'. In the old days, putting a star on the bench had often led to unrest.

THE BEGINNING OF THE OTTMAR HITZFELD ERA

Peace finally returned to Munich with the deliberate Ottmar Hitzfeld, who took over from Giovanni Trapattoni in the summer of 1998. From a pool of star players the successful coach (he'd won two league titles and the Champions League with Borussia Dortmund) managed to build a powerful team in which every player was used to his strengths. The French world-class defender Bixente Lizarazu and the Brazilian forward Giovane Elber responded particularly well, while midfield aces Effenberg and Matthäus pulled together instead of quarreling. Hitzfeld knew how to deal with star players and avoid turmoil. The former madhouse was now under control and success was the logical consequence: Bayern won the league by 15 points (!) over Leverkusen and reached the Champions League final for the first time since the competition had been re-branded.

Hitzfeld introduced a rotation policy under which star such as Mario Basler were sometimes benched.

In 1999 the opponent in the Champions League final was Manchester United.

LAST-GASP DEFEAT

The Champions League final against Manchester United was played on 26 May 1999 in Barcelona. At first everything went according to plan for Bayern. Set-piece specialist Mario Basler showed off his skills after only six minutes when he opened the scoring from a free kick. Subsequently Bayern appeared to effortlessly have the game and the opposition under control. Nothing could get in the way of victory, or so it seemed. Matthäus had already been substituted and regulation time was up. Then, abruptly, United turned the match around. Within a few seconds Beckham took two corners. The first was converted by Sheringham, the second by Solskjær. Bayern were beaten! Everybody had already been looking forward to the victory celebrations – now they were all on the ground, dejected. And as if frustration wasn't great enough already, Bayern also went on to lose the German Cup final shortly afterwards. Against old rivals Werder Bremen, the score was 1-1 after extra time. During the ensuing penalty shoot-out, team leaders Effenberg and Matthäus, of all people, wasted their spot-kicks.

'Weak as a bottle empty'

On 10 March 1998, Bayern coach Giovanni Trapattoni lost his composure during a press conference. After three consecutive defeats and heavy criticism from the players because of his cautious tactics, he had had enough. In broken German, he hit back: 'A coach is not an idiot. A coach sees what happens on field. There were two, three, four players in this match who were as weak as a bottle empty!' At the end of his outburst he said: 'I am having finished!' (Meaning: that's it.)

...ern players on the ground, ...ected after the Champions ...gue final defeat in 1999.

BAYERN'S BEST
THE STARS OF THE 1990s

THE BEST QUOTES

Olaf Thon: 'We don't let ourselves get nervous, and we also don't admit it.'
Giovanni Trapattoni on Thomas Strunz: 'Struuunz! How dare Strunz!'
Bayern treasurer Kurt Hegerich on Thomas Berthold, whom the club had suspended: 'The highest-paid golf pro after Bernhard Langer.'
Lothar Matthäus: 'We are a well-intrigued group.'
Lothar Matthäus again: 'One word led to another – we had nothing to say to each other.'
Jürgen Klinsmann: 'Rizzitelli and I are already a great trio . . . um, quartet'.
Mario Basler: 'Left wing, right wing – wherever I turned up, I was bad.'

In the 1990s, more players than ever before joined or left Bayern, and not all put in performances by which they could be remembered. Two of them, though, are particularly memorable: Lothar Matthäus and Jürgen Klinsmann.

Lothar Matthäus, born in the Franconian town Herzogenaurach where both Adidas and Puma are based, began his career in 1979 with Borussia

Lothar Matthäus

Mönchengladbach. In 1984 he moved to Bayern. Between 1988 and 1992, he played for Internazionale in Italy, then returned to Munich as a World Cup winner and two-time World Footballer of the Year (1990, 1991). On the pitch, Matthäus impressed as an outstanding distributor of the ball. Off the pitch, however, he made himself very unpopular with his team-mates due to his loose tongue. The German record international (150 caps) left FC Bayern in 2000 at the age of 39. These days, he is still waiting to have real success in his second career as a coach.

Germany striker **Jürgen Klinsmann** from Swabia began his professional career in the second division, with Kickers Stuttgart, before joining bigger local rivals VfB Stuttgart. He went on to have a lot of success at many clubs abroad (Inter, Monaco, Tottenham Hotspurs) before signing for Bayern in 1995. The perpetually smiling 1990 World Cup winner kept lifting silverware in Munich. With 15 goals (from 12 games!) he set a record during the 1995/96 UEFA Cup campaign. However, he left the club after a drawn-out dispute with Lothar Matthäus and moved to the United States to live there in 1998. In 2008, he returned to Munich to coach Bayern, but couldn't repeat the success he'd had as the national manager (guiding Germany to third place at the 2006 World Cup on home soil).

But there were many more players who left a positive and lasting impression. **Markus Babbel**, a born-and-bred Bavarian from Gilching who later played for Liverpool FC, marshalled the defence for six years. The defender **Thomas Helmer**, signed from Dortmund in 1992 for an estimated 8m Germans Marks (back then about £3m) – at that time a Bundesliga record. Five years later, he took over as team leader and captain from Lothar Matthäus. Midfielder **Thomas Strunz** was sometimes conspicuous by good performances and always by his bleached blond hair. He often ar-

Markus Babbel

Thomas Strunz

gued with coach Trapattoni, which the latter did not like one bit. Berlin-born **Christian Ziege** joined Bayern in 1990 as a 17-year-old and was a convincing and dynamic winger. **Christian Nerlinger**, who would briefly follow Uli Hoeness as Bayern's business manager, was an industrious midfielder who tirelessly closed gaps in case the stars lost possession. Blessed with great ball skills, **Olaf Thon**, who had started out at Schalke, was one of the last players who learned the game on the streets. Finally, older Bayern fans fondly remember the cheeky but lazy genius 'Super' **Mario Basler**, who liked to score directly from corner kicks.

There were other Bayern legends, such as Oliver Kahn, Stefan Effenberg, Mehmet Scholl and Giovane Elber, who started their careers in the 1990s. But their best years came only after the turn of the century.

Christian Ziege

Thomas Helmer

Christian Nerlinger

Olaf Thon

Jürgen Klinsmann

Mario Basler

'FOREVER NUMBER ONE'
FC Bayern
from 2000 to the present

Bundesliga champions 2000, 2001, 2003, 2005, 2006, 2008, 2010, 2013

DFB-Pokal winners 2000, 2003, 2005, 2006, 2008, 2010, 2013

Champions League winners 2001, 2013

Champions League finalists 2010, 2012

Intercontinental Cup winner 2001

A CLOSE TITLE RACE

Going into the last day of the 1999/2000 season, it was looking as if Bayer Leverkusen would become Bundesliga champions for the first time, as the team were three points ahead of Bayern. However, there was a rude awakening for the Leverkusen players in Unterhaching, a small suburb of Munich. They unexpectedly lost 2-0 against a team that was playing its first-ever Bundesliga season. Bayern, meanwhile, beat Werder Bremen 3-1 and climbed past Leverkusen to claim the title on goal difference. The team then went on to win the DFB-Pokal as well, thanks to another win against Werder Bremen, 3-0.

THE CLOSEST TITLE RACE

It seemed almost impossible – but the very next title race would be even closer. Bayern held a three-point lead over Schalke 04, but on the last matchday they fell behind 1-0 away at Hamburg in the 90th minute, while the final whistle had already sounded in Schalke, where the hosts had won 5-3 against Unterhaching. Deep into stoppage time, Bayern were awarded a free kick. It was to be the last goal attempt of the entire season. Bayern's defensive linchpin Patrick Andersson, a player with an extremely powerful shot, stepped up – and equalised! Bayern had done the impossible again and won the league by one point over Schalke. The celebration was indescribable. Goalkeeper Oliver Kahn couldn't contain himself, grabbed a corner flag and shook it like a madman.

Kahn and the corner flag after the dramatic 2001 league title.

Effenberg proudly lifts the Champions League trophy, and Samuel Kuffour kisses the Intercontinental Cup (below).

THREE SAVED PENALTIES

After this Bundesliga title – the third in a row – Bayern at last also brought European silverware back to Munich again. Their Champions League campaign was marked by getting revenge on Manchester United in the quarter-finals (1-0 and 2-1) and a triumph over Real Madrid in the semis (1-0 and 2-1). In the final in Milan on 23 May 2001, against the Spanish club FC Valencia, the Germans were considered favourites. And this time they made all predictions come true: fuelled by captain and midfielder Effenberg's irrepressible desire to succeed, Bayern prevailed! Valencia took the lead through a penalty, Effenberg made it 1-1 with another spot-kick. At the end of extra time, the score was still level and so the game went to penalties. Two Bayern players missed, but goalkeeper Oliver Kahn pushed himself to new heights and parried three shots with incredible saves. 5-4 on penalties – Bayern was the best team in Europe!

INTERCONTINENTAL CUP WINNERS

Towards the end of the year, a few months after the eagerly-awaited triumph in the Champions League, Bayern also went on to win the Intercontinental Cup, 1-0 against South American champions Boca Juniors (the goal was scored by Samuel Kuffour). Now they could consider themselves the best football team in the world!

The Bayern team that won the Champions League final on 23 May 2001

Scholl Salihamidzic Elber

Sagnol Lizarazu Hargreaves Effenberg

Kuffour Andersson Linke

Kahn

Jancker (for Sagnol), Zickler (for Elber) and Sergio (for Scholl) were brought on.

The opponent in the Champions League final was FC Valencia from Spain.

BAYERN'S BEST THE 2001 CHAMPIONS

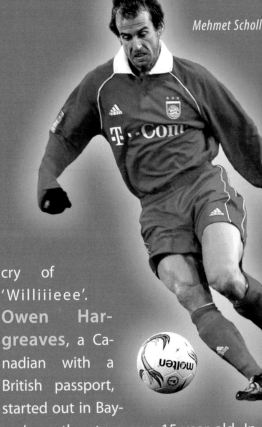

Mehmet Scholl

When he moved from Karlsruher SC to FC Bayern in 1994, **Oliver Kahn** had just been voted the Bundesliga's best goalkeeper. The goalkeeper, who had burning ambition and trained hard, was soon the 'face' of FC Bayern. No one could be quite as irate as him when it wasn't going well; nobody could be as wildly excited as him when the team won. At the 2002 World Cup in South Korea and Japan, he became the best goalkeeper in the world. This made it all the more bitter for Kahn when he had to make room for his rival Jens Lehmann four years later at the World Cup on home soil. At his club, however, Kahn was always undisputed and loved by the fans. When Bayern were having a bad spell, the supporters held up a banner with the words: 'Apart from Olli, you can all leave.'

The Swede **Patrik Andersson** was a cool leader of the Bayern defence. He was supported by **Samuel Kuffour**, a quick and sometimes rough man from Ghana, and by the inconspicuous but always reliable **Thomas Linke**. The short Basque **Bixente Lizarazu**, a World Cup winner with France in 1998, was one of the best left backs in the history of FC Bayern. For a long time, his partner on the right flank was **Willy Sagnol**, also a French international. His powerful runs down the wing made him a firm fan favourite, the crowd spurred him on with the rallying cry of 'Williiieee'.

Owen Hargreaves, a Canadian with a British passport, started out in Bayern's youth set-up as a 15-year-old. In April 2001 the hard-working midfielder made his first appearance with the pros and became a first-team regular. In May 2007, he signed for his dream club Manchester United, where he would be haunted by injuries.

Stefan Effenberg returned to FC Bayern in 1998. His first stint at the club (1991-92) had been not too fortunate, but now he became the undisputed midfield maestro and team leader. Nobody could lead a team quite like Effenberg and that is why he, together with Oliver Kahn, is regarded as the key to Bayern's success in 2001.

Mehmet Scholl was born Mehmet Yüksel and took his current surname from his mother's second husband. He moved from Karlsruhe to Munich, just as Oliver Kahn did. Scholl had excellent technique and was a superb set-piece specialist. He stayed in Munich for 15 years and is one of the best-loved Bayern players of all time. He was often

Oliver Kahn

plagued by injuries but never gave up. Today he works as a television pundit. The Brazilian **Giovane Elber** made a name for himself as a centre forward with VfB Stuttgart and moved to Bayern in 1997. Elber possessed silky skills, could get past defenders and was lethal in front of goal. He was hard to contain, because he could score with either foot and was also a threat in the air.

The powerful **Jens Jeremies** joined Bayern from local rivals 1860. 'Jerry' was a reliable holding midfielder, playing in front of the back four. In 2006 he had to end his career due to knee problems. The Bosnian **Hasan Salihamidzic**, nicknamed 'Brazzo' ('little fellow' in English) was indeed short but was feared by his opponents due to his fighting spirit.

THE SUBSTITUTES

The model athlete **Alexander Zickler** was never a proper goalscoring threat, but he stayed at FC Bayern for 13 years. (He later won the Golden Boot in

Austria playing for Red Bull Salzburg.) The beefy forward **Carsten Jancker** (he stood six feet four inches, weighed 92 kilograms and wore size 12 shoes) was noticeable for his bald head – and for the effort he put in. **Paulo Sergio**, a devout Christian, won the World Cup with Brazil in 1994 and was always useful in Bayern's attack.

During the Champions League campaign, several other men played a role and contributed to the triumph – for example **Michael Tarnat**, a man with a ferocious shot (73 mph), or the industrious midfielder **Thorsten Fink**.

Stefan Effenberg

Giovane Elber

...yern squad in 2001/02 (from left): Top row: Effenberg, Jancker, Santa Cruz, Sergio, Linke, di Salvo, Thiam, Hofmann, Tarnat, Zickler; ...e row: physio Gebhardt, Hoffmann, Binder; Jeremies, Pizarro, Wojciechowski, R. Kovac, Sagnol, Kuffour, assistant coach Henke, head coach ...d; bottom row: Fink, Scholl, Salihamidzic, N. Kovac, Wessels, Kahn, Dreher, Hargreaves, Lizarazu, Elber, rehabilitation expert Hauenstein.

55

NEW DOUBLES

During the last three seasons under Ottmar Hitzfeld – who worked in Munich for six consecutive years, longer than any Bayern coach before him – the club alternated between disappointment and success. The glory year of 2001 was followed by 2002 which brought no titles at all. Hitzfeld then rebuilt the team around midfield star Michael Ballack. In 2003, Bayern won another league and cup double. When things started to go downhill again in the following year, Ottmar Hitzfeld's time as coach had run out. His successor was Felix Magath. He led Bayern to back-to-back doubles (2005 and 2006). No coach and no club had ever achieved such a 'double double' before.

Michael Ballack, Bayern's new star player.

Felix Magath (right) followed Ottmar Hitzfeld (left) as coach.

He joined in 2003 and although his game was not always beautiful, he scored regularly: Dutch striker Roy Makaay.

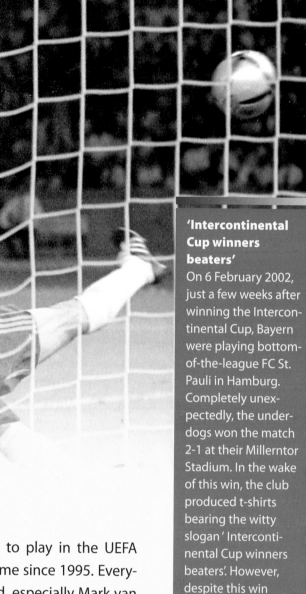

NOT UP TO SCRATCH IN EUROPE

Domestically, that is to say in the Bundesliga and the DFB-Pokal, Bayern remained the undisputed number one. On the European stage, however, the club was no longer able to reap success. Not even temporarily adopting white shirts, in order to more closely resemble mighty Real Madrid, helped Bayern.

Between 2002 and 2007, the team never made it past the quarter-finals in the Champions League, despite expensive new signings, such as Dutch predator Roy Makaay. A low point was the 2002/03 season when Bayern earned only two points in the group stage and were eliminated early. Their bogey team was AC Milan, who repeatedly knocked Bayern out of the competition. Particularly the delicate striker Filippo Inzaghi hurt the Germans: he scored six goals in five games against FC Bayern. When, in 2007, Bayern only came 4th in the Bun-

desliga, they had to play in the UEFA Cup for the first time since 1995. Everyone was frustrated, especially Mark van Bommel, who derisively called that competition the 'Fiat Punto Clio Cup'.

'Intercontinental Cup winners beaters'

On 6 February 2002, just a few weeks after winning the Intercontinental Cup, Bayern were playing bottom-of-the-league FC St. Pauli in Hamburg. Completely unexpectedly, the underdogs won the match 2-1 at their Millerntor Stadium. In the wake of this win, the club produced t-shirts bearing the witty slogan 'Intercontinental Cup winners beaters'. However, despite this win St. Pauli couldn't avoid relegation that season.

SUPERSTARS IN BAYERN SHIRTS

For decades, Uli Hoeness categorically refused to purchase super-expensive stars. He didn't want Bayern to sink into debt, as had happened to competitors Borussia Dortmund. But because Bayern were no longer among the best in the Champions League, the club decided to buy new players for the record total sum of more than 80m Euros (£54m) in the summer of 2007. Stars such as striker Miroslav Klose from Werder Bremen, the Italian World Cup winner Luca Toni and the French dribbler Franck Ribéry arrived. On Ribéry alone, who became the most expensive Bayern player until that time, the club spent 25 million Euros (£17m).

NEW SUCCESS, OLD SHORTCOMINGS

Ribéry, Toni and their team-mates played well and had success. Bayern won another double in 2008, wrapping up their 21st national championship as early as matchday 31 and winning their 14th DFB-Pokal 2-1 against Borussia Dortmund. In Europe, though, things were not going well. In the UEFA Cup, FC Bayern played some exciting games but were ultimately eliminated in the semi-finals by Zenit St. Petersburg, losing the second leg in Russia by a depressing 4-0 scoreline.

Expensive big-name transfers (from l to r): Franck Ribéry, Miroslav Klose, Luca Toni.

Arjen Robben (left), Mario Gomez

THE SURPRISE COACH

For the 2008/09 season, Bayern did not sign any new star players but a new coach: Jürgen Klinsmann. As Germany manager, the 1990 World Cup winner and former Bayern player had led the national team to a great 3rd place at the 2006 World Cup. Klinsmann wanted Bayern to have success and at the same time play beautiful football. But his team rarely did that. In the Bundesliga, FC Bayern saw VfL Wolfsburg climb into first place, and in the DFB-Pokal, the German cup, they were knocked out by Leverkusen. Only in the Champions League did it appear to go well. Bayern finished first during the group stage and then beat Sporting from Lisbon 12-1 on aggregate in the round of 16. However, Klinsmann's team was overmatched against FC Barcelona in the quarter-finals, losing the first leg 4-0. Bayern drew the second leg 1-1 at home, but never stood a chance of going through.

A NEW APPROACH

Ahead of the 2009/10 season, Bayern changed coaches again and settled on the experienced Louis van Gaal. The Dutchman, who had won major trophies with Ajax Amsterdam and Barcelona, was signed to bring the silverware that had eluded his predecessor to Munich. To this end he acquired two expensive stars – striker Mario Gomez from VfB Stuttgart cost 35m Euros (£31m), which set a new transfer record, while the fast dribbler Arjen Robben was signed shortly after the beginning of the season from Real Madrid for 24m Euros (£21m). He immediately struck up such a good partnership with Ribéry that people were soon raving about the new dream duo 'Robbéry'. But van Gaal also put his trust in young players that had come up through the youth ranks: offensive midfielder Thomas Müller and centre back Holger Badstuber became first-team regulars.

'I want to make every player a little bit better every day,' Jürgen Klinsmann announced when he took over as Bayern coach. Ten months later not a single player had improved. In fact, there was hardly a player who was as good as he'd been the previous year. Klinsmann's tenure ended early.

The idiosyncratic coach Louis van Gaal.

BAYERN'S BEST
THE STARS 2001–2011

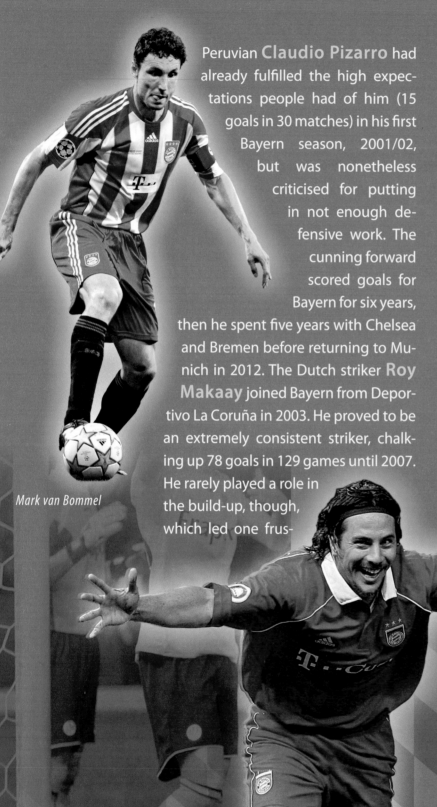

Peruvian Claudio Pizarro had already fulfilled the high expectations people had of him (15 goals in 30 matches) in his first Bayern season, 2001/02, but was nonetheless criticised for putting in not enough defensive work. The cunning forward scored goals for Bayern for six years, then he spent five years with Chelsea and Bremen before returning to Munich in 2012. The Dutch striker Roy Makaay joined Bayern from Deportivo La Coruña in 2003. He proved to be an extremely consistent striker, chalking up 78 goals in 129 games until 2007. He rarely played a role in the build-up, though, which led one frus-

Mark van Bommel

trated opponent to complain: 'He almost never has the ball, but when he does, it's too late – he's already scored.' Lukas Podolski moved to Bayern after the 2006 World Cup (and as a big hero in his native Cologne) to join up with his good mate Bastian Schweinsteiger. Although he was a regular starting player for Germany, 'Poldi' never really settled down in Munich and returned to Cologne in 2009 (he's now playing for Arsenal). Miroslav Klose is looking to better Gerd Müller's scoring record for the national team. Comfortable on the ball, strong in the air and known for celebrating goals with a somersault, Klose did not enjoy a smooth ride at Bayern between 2007 and 2011, though.

Centre forward Luca Toni, a 2006 World Cup winner with Italy, was the Bundesliga's top goalscorer with 24 goals in his very first season at Bayern in 2007/08. But then things deteriorated and at the end of December 2009, he moved to Roma in Italy. Michael Ballack, who joined from Bayer Leverkusen in 2002/03 and later captained the national team, quickly proved to be the pivotal player everyone had expected him to be. The tall, elegant player was widely regarded one of the most dangerous midfielders in the world, scoring a goal almost every

Claudio Pizarro

other match during his four years with Bayern – often with his head.

Another player who moved to Bayern from Leverkusen was the Brazilian **Zé Roberto**, who spent six years in Munich. The man with the strong left foot considered his ball skills a 'gift from God' and his delightful game could indeed sometimes appear otherworldly. Midfielder **Mark van Bommel,** a Dutch international, was a key player and team leader for five years until his departure in January 2011. If need be, he could be quite ruthless. The Argentinian **Martín Demichelis** put in many good performances in his seven years (2003–10) at the heart of the defence. The Brazilian **Lúcio** began his career as a striker but then emerged as one of the best centre backs in the world. He was feared for his winning mentality and also for his forays deep into the opponent's half (in these moments it told that he had once been a forward). After five years as a Bayern mainstay he moved to Inter in 2009. One attacking player who was very popular with fans was **Ivica Olić.** The mobile Croatian was always working very hard for the team and darted around the opponent's penalty area like a wind-up toy. He did particularly well on the European stage, but since he couldn't hold down a regular place in the starting XI, he left for VfL Wolfsburg in the summer of 2012.

Lúcio

Podolski

Left: Michael Ballack, right: Zé Roberto

VICTORY WITH FIGHTING SPIRIT, SKILL AND SMARTS

Louis van Gaal's team needed quite a while before it got going. The coach had a clear vision: the players should move on the pitch according to his plan and create scoring opportunities by stringing passes together. Since this strategy did not work at first, there were several bitter defeats at the beginning of the season. Only towards the end of November 2009 did Bayern begin to win crucial games in the Bundesliga and the Champions League by never losing belief and fighting spirit, no matter how difficult the situation. The players eventually mastered the 'positional play' van Gaal demanded and executed it almost perfectly. The key players were Bastian Schweinsteiger and Mark van Bommel, who built from the rear, and Arjen Robben, Ivica Olić and Thomas Müller, who took turns scoring crucial goals.

LEAGUE CHAMPIONSHIP 2010

The toughest rival in the Bundeliga was Schalke, coached by the former Bayern gaffer Felix Magath. For all practical purposes, the title race was decided on matchday 29, as Bayern won 2-1 at Schalke. The club's 22nd national championship was sealed on the penultimate day, when Schalke lost 2-0 to Bremen and Bayern won 3-1 against Bochum, with Müller having a hat-trick, since van Gaal's team now held a three-point lead and the much better goal difference.

Triumphs in 2010: Schweinsteiger celebrates the Bundesliga title, Robben (top right) the German cup.

DFB-Pokal Winners 2010

En route to the final, Bayern beat SpVgg Neckarelz (3-1), Rot-Weiss Oberhausen (5-0), Eintracht Frankfurt (4-0), SpVgg Greuther Fürth (6-2) and, in the semi-final, FC Schalke 04 (1-0 AET). Arjen Robben decided this game with a terrific solo run in extra time. By comparison, the final itself wasn't much of a contest. Robben, Olić, Ribéry and Schweinsteiger were on target for a great Bayern side that won 4-0 and played opponents Werder Bremen off the park.

Champions League Final 2010

At first things were not looking good for Bayern in Europe. In the group stage, only a terrific 4-1 win in the final match at Juventus secured their passage to the next round. From then on, though, Bayern may have looked shaky on occasion but never fell. In both the round of 16 (against Fiorentina from Italy) and the quarter-finals (against old rivals Manchester United) Bayern only went through on the away-goals rule. The game in Manchester was particularly close, because Bayern fell behind 3-0, before Olić and Robben – with a per-

fect volley – pulled two goals back to see the Germans through. In the semi-finals against Olympique Lyonnais (1-0 and 3-0) Bayern demonstrated almost perfect football. The outstanding player of the second leg was Ivica Olić, who scored all three goals.

In the final against Inter, a team built around an extremely strong defence, the dream of winning the Champions League collapsed. As was their wont, Bayern tried to outplay their opponents by having a lot of ball possession, but they rarely found a chink in Inter's armour and had very few chances. Inter sat back and hoped to hit Bayern on the break. They did this twice and Bayern lost the final 2-0. Still, there was reason to celebrate, for the team had played a fantastic season.

The opponent in the 2010 final was Inter.

To his wife with love: Olić kisses his wedding ring after every goal.

Mario Gomez won the 2011 Golden Boot with 28 goals. In 2012, he scored 26 goals and finished second behind Schalke's Huntelaar (29 goals).

coach van Gaal constantly quarrelled with president Uli Hoeness and made some odd decisions, for instance benching the veteran goalkeeper Butt and replacing him with the untried youngster Kraft. Finally, the Dutchman was sacked shortly before the end of the season. His assistant Andries Jonker at least guided the team to a 3rd-place finish.

An experienced coach was signed for the new season, as Bayern brought back Jupp Heynckes. He felt the most pressing task was to bolster Bayern's shaky defence with some new signings – Germany goalkeeper Manuel Neuer plus defenders Jérôme Boateng and Rafinha.

2011: New Beginning With Jupp Heynckes

During the 2010/11 season, all of a sudden things were not going well for FC Bayern anymore. The team rarely played good football and frequently lost. In the Champions League there was yet another defeat at the hands of Inter, this time as early as the round of 16. In the domestic cup, the semi-finals were as good as it got (Schalke won 1-0). And the team's showings in the Bundesliga were equally mediocre. On top of it,

2012: Problems After The Winter Break

At the start of the 2011/12 Bundesliga season, Bayern lost 1-0 at home against Borussia Mönchengladbach, a team that had almost been relegated the previous season. But then the team embarked on a winning run. At the end of the first half of the season, Bayern topped the table by three points. This seemed to be a good omen, because it marked the 16th time Bayern had been in first place when the winter break began – and had

No Neuer

Although Germany goalkeeper Manuel Neuer had proved his class during the 2010 World Cup, many Bayern fans had doubts about his signing. They were bothered by the fact that he had always maintained to be a big Schalke fan. On banners they declared they needed 'No Neuer' ('Neuer' translates as 'new one'). But the protests died down quickly when the world-class goalkeeper proved to be a real asset to the team.

Utter shock: Arjen Robben after his wasted penalty against Dortmund. Bayern's 1-0 defeat decided the title race.

subsequently won the league title in 14 of those cases. But this time there were some bitter defeats early into the second half of the season, as Borussia Dortmund climbed past Bayern and built up a seven-point lead. But Bayern bounced back and began a new winning run. On matchday 30, as Bayern travelled to Dortmund, they trailed the league leaders by just three points. The game was practically a final. And it was very close. Lewandowski gave Dortmund the lead with a back-heeled goal. Robben had the chance to equalise from the penalty spot, but he missed and then also wasted another great chance shortly before the final whistle. This unlucky 1-0 defeat and the following scoreless draw at home against Mainz ended all title hopes. For the tenth time in the club's history, Bayern finished a Bundesliga season as runners-up.

had now lost four games straight. They desperately wanted to break this spell, but it was not to be. Just three minutes into game, the Japanese Kagawa (now with Manchester United) caught the Bayern defence unaware and opened the scoring. Arjen Robben brought the Reds back into the game with a converted penalty. But while Bayern enjoyed the bulk of possession, the goals were scored by Dortmund. Hummels converted a penalty and Lewandowski put a Kagawa cross away – at half-time the score was 3-1. After the restart, Lewandowski scored two more goals, while only Franck Ribéry found the target for Bayern. The final result was 5-2. It was an extremely bitter defeat, caused by a lot of mistakes in defence.

The German cup semi-final: Neuer saves the deciding penalty.

Play-offs against Zürich

In this season, only the Bundesliga champions and the runners-up won direct qualification to the Champions League. Third-placed Bayern had to qualify through two-legged play-offs in which they met the Swiss runners-up, FC Zürich. With two victories (2-0 and 1-0) Bayern easily went through.

12 May 2012: Cup Shock in Berlin

Almost exactly a month after the bitter defeat in Dortmund, Bayern had the chance to take revenge and again a title was at stake, this time the DFB-Pokal. Heynckes's team had reached the final in Berlin after eliminating Borussia Mönchengladbach on penalties in the semis. Now Bayern faced Borussia Dortmund again, a team against which they

Disappointed: Bastian Schweinsteiger during the German cup final.

The celebrations following Schweinsteiger's penalty in Madrid: Bayern have reached the 2012 Champions League final.

Bestia Negra

At Real Madrid, they call Bayern 'la bestia negra', the black beast, which is the Spanish expression for a bogey team. Out of 20 European games against Real, Bayern won eleven and lost only seven. If you consider the 2012 penalty shoot-out win another victory (the game itself had ended in a 2-1 defeat), then the score is even 12-6. The record European Cup winners from Madrid (nine titles!) have never struggled quite as much against any other club.

2012: THE ROAD TO THE FINAL AT HOME

There remained one big hope for FC Bayern in the cursed 2011/12 season: the Champions League. The final would be held in Munich, in Bayern's own Allianz Arena. Naturally, the team was determined to reach this final and enjoy the home advantage. In the group stage, Bayern triumphed rather easily over strong opposition – Villareal, Manchester City and Napoli. In the knockout rounds they eliminated FC Basel and Olympique Marseille. Then, in the semi-finals against Real Madrid, who were fielding superstar Cristiano Ronaldo and the two German internationals Mesut Özil and Sami Khedira, things got really exciting and tense.

In the 17th minute of the first leg, played in the Allianz Arena, Ribéry put away a rebound, making it 1-0. In the 53rd minute, Özil equalised from a counterattack. Even though Bayern thoroughly dominated the game, they only scored through Gomez in the very last minute, winning 2-1. In the return game, in the cauldron of Madrid's Bernabéu Stadium, Bayern were under enormous pressure right from the start. After only 14 minutes they were down 2-0, Ronaldo having scored a brace. Still, Bayern did not let themselves be discouraged and managed to pull one back with a Robben penalty. There were no goals in extra time and so the tie was decided in a penalty shoot-out. After two Bayern players and three opponents had failed to convert their attempts, Bastian Schweinsteiger became the hero: with nerves of steel he put Bayern's fifth and deciding penalty away. The Reds were in the final in Munich!

19 MAY 2012: THE WORST OF ALL HOME DEFEATS

In their own stadium, Bayern met Chelsea, who had surprisingly knocked out Barcelona's wonder team. The Blues were an unpredictable opponent, but Bayern were still considered the clear favourites. Actually, it almost seemed as if triumph in the Allianz Arena would be just a matter of patience. Bayern were superior in every regard right from the beginning and created a plethora of opportunities against extremely defensive Blues. But the goals just wouldn't come. It wasn't until the 83rd minute that the spell was finally broken. From a Toni Kroos cross, Thomas Müller headed the ball goalwards. It took a bounce and

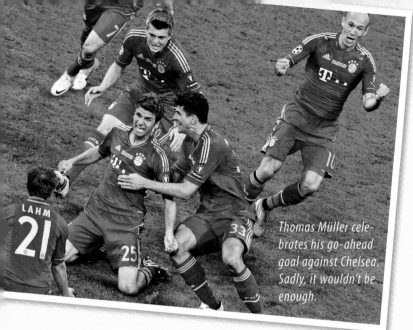

Thomas Müller celebrates his go-ahead goal against Chelsea. Sadly, it wouldn't be enough.

Didier Drogba celebrates: the 34-year-old striker from the Ivory Coast plays the greatest game of his life and wins the final for his team.

flew over the fists of goalkeeper Cech and against the underside of the crossbar – from where it rebounded into the net. It was a more than deserved lead and Bayern were looking like the sure winners.

But minutes later, the shock came. Chelsea won their first corner of the game. Didier Drogba raced into the box and headed the ball forcefully past Manuel Neuer into the triangle to tie the final at 1-1. And so the game went to extra time. Bayern kept throwing everything forward and Robben had the great chance to win the game – but Cech saved his penalty. At the final whistle, the dominating Bayern had had 19 attempts at goal (Chelsea had 6) and won 20 corners (the Blues just one), but the score was still 1-1. Just as in the semi-finals, penalties would have to decide. The shoot-out started well, because Manuel Neuer saved, while Lahm and Gomez scored. But then Olić missed and Chelsea drew level. Schweinsteiger had Cech beaten – but saw the ball hit the post. Finally, Drogba took a run-up and converted the last penalty of the night. Game over. It was the worst home defeat in the history of FC Bayern.

The Bayern players were inconsolable after the final whistle. But they didn't have to feel embarrassed. They were the much better team and only lost on account of bad luck – and the clinical Drogba.

Statements about the 'drama at home'

'When you're as dominant as we were, you have to win.'
Philipp Lahm

'We can't say everything is okay if we lose three finals. I'm not one to put up with that.'
President Uli Hoeness

A rarity: Jérôme Boateng scores a goal. His header gave Bayern a 3-2 win against Fortuna Düsseldorf on matchday 25 – and a 20-point lead in the league!

On 30 March 2013, everything fell into place, as Bayern won 9-2 against HSV (Hamburg). The great poacher Claudio Pizarro had four goals, scoring Bayern's sixth with a back-heeler.

2012/13: THE STRONGEST BAYERN TEAM OF ALL TIME

For the 2012/13 campaign, the Bundesliga's 50th anniversary season, Bayern bolstered their squad once more. The Spaniard Javi Martinez, a midfield strategist of the highest class, was bought for the new record transfer fee of 40m Euros (£34m). The Brazilian Dante was signed to shore up defence. The striker Mario Mandzukić, old friend Claudio Pizarro and the lively Xherdan Shaquiri increased Bayern's options upfront and on the wings. Every new signing would turn out to be a hit. Another very important element was that coach Heynckes taught the mavericks Ribéry and Robben how to track back and help the defence. From now on, both would still thrill crowds with their solo runs, but they would also work hard for the team. Team leaders Schweinsteiger and Lahm consistently played at the highest level, the same went for younger players such as Müller, Kroos, Boateng and Alaba. Goalkeeper Neuer was, as usual, a reliable number one. In fact, he didn't get much work: while Bayern scored goal upon goal from clever moves or fast counterattacks upfront, they were also so solid at the back that almost every opponent was completely helpless.

THE SEASON OF RECORDS

From the very first matchday, Bayern let rip. Eight wins from the first eight games set a new Bundesliga record for the start of the season. Three times, against Stuttgart, Düsseldorf and Hannover, Bayern won by a five-goal margin. Soon they were setting more records: after the first half of the season, as the Bundesliga went into its traditional winter break, Bayern had conceded only one single goal away from home!

When play resumed, Bayern continued where they had left off. On matchday 25, after a somewhat difficult 3-2 against Fortuna Düsseldorf, they already held a 20-point lead. On matchday 27, they demolished Hamburg 9-2 and came close to setting a new Bundesliga scoring record (which stands at 12-0). And on matchday 28, they won the league with a 1-0 win in Frankfurt. It set yet another record: never before had the Bundesliga title been decided so early! At the end of this fantastic season, Bayern was the champion with the largest lead of all time (25 points), the most points in all (91), and the best goal difference (+80) as well as the fewest goals conceded (18). And these are just a few of the records they broke en route to their 23rd national championship (see p. 7).

7-0 TRIUMPH AGAINST BARCELONA

In the group stage of the Champions League, Bayern came first in their group, ahead of Valencia. In the round of 16, they briefly ran into problems against Arsenal, as Bayern won the away leg 3-1, which caused overconfidence and led to a 2-0 defeat at home. In the quarter-finals, Bayern dominated Italian champions Juventus and convincingly won both legs 2-0. Now, it seemed, a stern test awaited them, because their opponents in the semi-finals were mighty Barcelona with their superstar Lionel Messi. It turned into a marvellous triumph. In the first leg, at the Allianz Arena, Bayern were in command and had many chances. Thomas Müller opened the scoring with a header in the 25th minute. In the second half, Gomez, Robben and Müller added three goals for a final score of 4-0. A fantastic Bayern team had played 'Barça' off the park with enthusiasm and pace, with purpose and inspiration, with team spirit and athleticism. In the second leg in Barcelona, Bayern kept their focus and were always in the driver's seat, humiliating their opponents 3-0. Thus the aggregate result against what had been regarded the best team in the world was 7-0!

The champions form a pyramid: Franck Ribéry, reserve goalkeeper Tom Starke and captain Philipp Lahm celebrate the 23rd German championship.

Semi-final triumph in the Champions League: Thomas Müller has just crowned his phenomenal performance against Barcelona with the goal that made it 4-0.

Manuel Neuer made some world-class saves in the Wembley final. Here he denies Borussia's striker Robert Lewandowski.

The Wembley final: after a fine dribble, Robben sneaks the ball past Borussia goalkeeper Weidenfeller and into the net with his left foot to score the winning goal.

25 May 2013: Champions At Wembley

For the first time ever, there was an all-German final in the Champions League, because Bayern's opponents were Borussia Dortmund. The Reds were considered the favourites, as Dortmund had needed some luck against Malaga and Real Madrid to reach this final. Still, it would certainly be an exciting game. After all, Bayern had suffered five defeats in their last seven games against Dortmund. However, after a long barren spell, an Arjen Robben goal had finally given Bayern a win against their rivals in the quarter-finals of the German cup on 27 February.

The Wembley final was another close, thrilling game. Borussia Dortmund got off to a great start and Manuel Neuer had to make a string of excellent saves to prevent his team from falling behind. But then, gradually, Schweinsteiger and his men began to make their presence felt. Arjen Robben had a few superb chances but could not beat the excellent Weidenfeller in Dortmund's goal. Finally, after the restart, an aggressive Bayern team, attacking with pace over the wings, seized control of the game. In the 60th minute, Mandzukić scored the opening goal, having been set up by Ribéry and Robben.

The 2013 Champions League winners

Mandzukić**

Ribéry* T. Müller Robben

Javi Martinez Schweinsteiger

Alaba Dante Boateng Lahm

Neuer

*90+1 Luiz Gustavo, **90+4 Gomez

WINNERS
UEFA CHAMPIONS LEAGUE 2012/13

But Borussia came back when the referee awarded Dortmund a penalty for Dante's foul on Reus and Gündogan equalised from the spot. However, Bayern remained the better team. With one minute left on the clock, Arjen Robben finally had his moment in the spotlight. Boateng fed Ribéry with a long pass, the Frenchman kept possession even though he was challenged by defenders, then he back-heeled the ball into Robben's path. Robben went past Hummels and Subotić and calmly made it 2-1. It was the last goal of the night. Bayern were finally champions of Europe and could take the 'cup with the big ears' back to Munich!

Bayern have reached their goal, they are winners of the 2013 Champions League!

1 June 2013: Completing The First Treble

Now there was only one trophy missing from Bayern's silverware collection in 2013, the DFB-Pokal. After an easy 6-1 win over VfL Wolfsburg in the semi-finals, only rank outsiders VfB Stuttgart stood between Bayern and a historic treble. In the final in Berlin, the Swabians held their own until the 37th minute, when the referee pointed to the spot after Lahm had been brought down. Thomas Müller scored to give Bayern the lead. In the second half, striker Mario Gomez, who had been given a rare berth in the starting XI, added two more to make it 3-0. Bayern appeared to be cruising, but Stuttgart never gave up and pulled back two goals. It wasn't enough. A 3-2 win meant Bayern had crowned their greatest-ever season with yet another title. It was the first treble in German football history!

Coach Jupp Heynckes, the 68-year-old 'architect' of the historic treble, bids farewell after the most successful Bayern season of all time, clutching the German cup.

BAYERN'S BEST
TODAY'S STARS

GOALKEEPERS

Since 2011, one of the best goalkeepers in the world is between the sticks for Bayern, Germany's number one Manuel Neuer (1). The 2009 Under-21 European champion has lightning-fast reflexes and calmly deals with crosses. He has a good positional sense and is always in command. His particular speciality is instigating swift counter-attacks with his long throws. In 2011, he was voted 'Germany's Footballer of the Year' in recognition of his outstanding performances. In 2012, the former Hoffenheim player Tom Starke (22) replaced Hans Jörg Butt (who finished his career) as Bayern's number two goalkeeper. The experienced stand-in proved he is a reliable sub with several appearances in the Bundesliga and in the German cup. Also under contract, to learn from Neuer and Starke, is the young hopeful Lukas Raeder (32).

Famous for his long throws: Bayern keeper Manuel Neuer

DEFENCE

The diminutive wing back Philipp Lahm (21) joined Bayern as a twelve-year-old from the small Munich club FT Gern. As a professional he then spent some time at Stuttgart. Today, as captain of the national team and of FC Bayern, he is one of the most respected German footballers. Lahm not only convinces on the pitch with excellent performances, he can also express himself well in front of cameras and microphones and has even written a book.

Since Lahm was used mostly at left back, Bayern signed the small Brazilian Rafinha (13) as right back in 2011. Although he is agile and always fired-up, he never managed to become a regular. These days, Lahm is usually playing on the right flank, because young David Alaba (27) has put in convincing performances at left back. A trained midfielder who was pulled back into defence, Alaba covers a lot of ground and is comfortable on the ball. He has also struck up a perfect partnership with Franck Ribéry, who plays in front of him. Alaba grew up as the son of a Philippino mother and a Nigerian father in Vienna. In 2009, at the age of 17, he became the youngest Austrian international of all time.

Another option at the full back position is Diego Contento (26). He came up through the Bayern youth ranks and is particularly good in one-on-ones.

David Alaba

Holger Badstuber and Jérôme Boateng

Daniel van Buyten

In 2011, the German international **Jérôme Boateng** (17) was signed for a transfer fee of 13.5m Euros (£11.7m). The son of a Ghanaian grew up in Berlin and has his strengths as a central defender. The half-brother of Kevin-Prince Boateng (AC Milan) is elegant and at the same time strong as an ox. In 2009 he won the Under-21 European Championships with Germany.

Even though he's still rough around the edges, **Holger Badstuber** (28) is a regular in the heart of Bayern's defence since 2009/10. For both club and country, the enormously reliable left-footed player impresses with calmness, perfect positional play and pinpoint accurate passes in the build-up. In 2012/13, **Daniel van Buyten** (5) was supposed to be just a substitute but saw plenty of action nonetheless. On a good day, the giant is a central defender hardly an opponent can get past. Aside from that, he is an unusually prolific goalscorer for a defensive player, particularly from corners. The Brazilian **Dante** (4), a firm fan favourite in Mönchengladbach, won a starting place in central defence on the very first matchday of the 2012/13 season. The man with the striking mop of hair, who captivates with his commanding presence, his vision and his strength in the air, has since become a Brazilian international. Young **Jan Kirchhoff** (15) joined Bayern in the summer of 2013 from Mainz and will have to fight one of the established centre backs for a starting place.

Dante

Skipper Philipp Lahm is equally good at left back and right back.

BAYERN'S BEST
TODAY'S STARS

He not only marshals the defence but also instigates attacks: Bastian Schwein-steiger

MIDFIELD & ATTACK

Bastian Schweinsteiger (31), born in Kolbermoor in Upper Bavaria, can read the game, is a great passer of the ball and as such the heart and soul of both Bayern and the national team. As a holding midfielder in front of the back four, he organises the defence but is also central to the build-up and thus the offence. Schweinsteiger is not only the team's pivotal player in every situation but also its emotional leader. After the long-time team leader Mark van Bommel left Bayern in 2011, the creative and versatile Brazilian **Luiz Gustavo** (30) was signed as his replacement. The elegant midfielder is a good ball winner and can instigate attacks, he was Schweinsteiger's regular partner until coach Jupp Heynckes was so convinced by the qualities of the defensive midfielder **Javier Martinez** (8) that he wanted to get him at any cost. In the summer of 2012, Bayern parted with the German record sum of 40m Euros (£32m) to sign Martinez from Athletic Bilbao. The tall, slender Spaniard has since shown that he is worth every cent: his positional play is smart, he is strong in one-on-ones, an outstanding header of the ball, reliable and deft in the build-up.

By comparison, another midfielder cost Bayern nothing at all: the enormously talented **Pierre-Emile Hojbjerg** (34). At 17 years and 251 days of age, he replaced David Alaba as the youngest Bayern player of all time. Other up-and-coming players are the forwards **Patrick Weihrauch** (20) **and Mitchell Weiser** (23). Blessed with great technical ability, the German international **Toni Kroos** **(39)** is a dead-ball specialist and playmaker who was loaned out to Leverkusen to learn before he was given a Bayern shirt in 2010. If he's used in the hole behind the strikers, his vision and passing create scoring opportunities. If he's playing alongside Schweinsteiger in front of the defence, he builds from the rear and sets up the forwards.

The best quotes

'When Javi Martinez was signed, nobody knew him. Franz Beckenbauer thought he was a coffee brand.'
Jupp Heynckes

'I crapped my pants a bit in the first ten minutes.'
Pierre-Emile Hojbjerg on his Bundesliga debut.

Javier Martinez

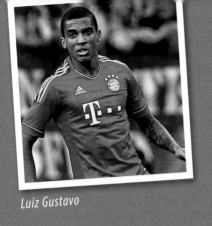

Luiz Gustavo

Franck Ribéry (7), the French whirlwind on the left wing, was given the shirt with Mehmet Scholl's number in 2007. Just as Scholl had done, he dazzles with silky skills and a bag of tricks. He is also extremely fast on the first few yards and makes opponents look sluggish. In the past, he was almost a classic, traditional winger, but he's since learned to take on defensive tasks if possession is lost. Since 2009, Ribéry has been partnered on the right flank by **Arjen Robben** (10). The Dutchman, another fast and skilled dribbler, is a very similar type of player. His signature move is running down the right wing, then sharply cutting inside and having a shot at goal with his dangerous left foot. In this way, Robben has scored many a goal for Bayern. This much is clear: with 'Robbéry' on the wings, Bayern can trouble any defence.

A fast and strong dribbler:
Arjen Robben

Sublime skills: the Frenchman
Franck Ribéry

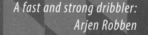

Toni Kroos

BAYERN'S BEST
TODAY'S STARS

MIDFIELD & ATTACK

As an old-school centre forward, Mario Gomez was one of the most successful Bayern strikers of all time (a Golden Boot winner in 2011). But the more versatile and multi-faceted Bayern's attacking play became, the more often Gomez was benched. In the summer of 2013, he left the club and signed with Fiorentina. In his place came an entirely different type of player but one which new coach Pep Guardiola desperately wanted to have – young **Thiago Alcantara** (6) from Guardiola's former club Barcelona. Bayern paid 25m Euros (£20m) to secure the services of Spain's Under-21 captain who can play any position in midfield and even in attack. Thiago is technically strong and a goal-scoring threat.

Always genial and a master of the good-natured quip, **Thomas Müller** (25) started out with small TSV Pähl before joining Bayern's youth set-up. The namesake of Bayern's legendary striker Gerd Müller loves to cover a lot of ground and rose from the reserves to the national team in record time. At the beginning of 2009, he was still playing for Bayern's second team, in the same year he became a regular Bundesliga player and one summer later, at the 2010 World Cup, he finishing joint-top of the scoring charts with five goals. The lanky forward, whose moves sometimes look comical, is an extremely unpredictable, instinctive football player. He covers the entire pitch and anticipates situations well thanks to his spatial awareness. Again and again, he will appear in unexpected places and score out of the blue.

Since it was becoming apparent during the 2011/12 season that Bayern's offence was too one-dimensional, the club decided to add attacking power. One new signing was the Croatian

Elegant:
Thomas Müller.

'NOTHING WILL DRIVE ME AWAY FROM FC BAYERN.'
Thomas Müller

Mario Mandzukic

Xherdan Shaqiri

Claudio Pizarro

Thiago Alcantara

Mario Mandzukić (9), who was lured away from VfL Wolfsburg for 13m Euros (£10m). The hard-working forward was an immediate hit, particularly due to his qualities as a team player. He tracked back if possession was lost, linked up well with the midfielders, created chances for others and scored himself. **Claudio Pizarro** (14) is always there when needed. The experienced Peruvian, who joined from Werder Bremen at the advanced footballing age of 33, is still a powerful threat to goal. If things are not going so well, he is always an option as a super-sub. During the 2012/13 season, the young Kosovar Albanian and Swiss international **Xherdan Shaqiri** (11) also proved that he is a quality player – a lively and dynamic offensive midfielder. For the 2013/14 season, the arguably greatest talent in German football, the former Dortmund player **Mario Götze** (19), is yet another highlight in the already star-studded Bayern squad. The highly gifted wizard has been compared to Barcelona's star Lionel Messi. That's high praise, but Götze indeed has everything it takes to one day become the world's best footballer.

Coach Pep Guardiola explains his strategy to Mario Götze.

EVERYTHING ABOUT FC BAYERN

About 35 million spectators at Bundesliga home games since promotion in 1965

Over 20 million self-professed Bayern fans

Some 3 million spectators per season

Average home attendance: 71,000

Roughly 240,000 fan-club members

Over 200,000 club members

More than 3,200 Bayern fan clubs

The oldest Bayern logo is the flag; the ornate lettering was effective into the 1950s. The oval with the diamonds was worn on the shirts as far back as Beckenbauer's time.

THE BAYERN LOGO

Every football club has a logo, a kind of emblem, and every German fan knows the Bayern Munich logo: in the middle is the Bavarian flag, which is surrounded by a red circle in which the name of the club appears in white. Up until a few years ago, the letters 'e.V', which stand for 'registered association', also appeared in the red circle. Since 2002, however, the professional football division of FC Bayern is no longer a registered association but has been made a public limited company. Therefore the 'e.V.' had to be removed from the logo. FC Bayern's logo did not always look like this. Over the years the crest on the footballers' shirts has changed over and again. The colour red did not appear in the first logo in 1900. The founders of the club had originally chosen the Bavarian colours white and blue as the club colours.

Even your face can be made up to show off the Bayern logo.

Wearing the FC Bayern logo on his clothing, this shows his affinity for the club.

THE HISTORY OF THE FOOTBALL CREST

The logos of football clubs are the modern version of the medieval coat of arms. The crests of knights – and also of tradesmen and cities – were very important, because many people could not read at that time. A crest's meaning, though, was instantly understood by everyone. It's the same today: if you're a Bayern fan, just put the logo on your clothes and you don't have to explain anything. The logo is displayed on all fan merchandise; every fan has at least one piece of fan clothing, and at fan club meetings a large flag usually hangs on the wall.

The white and blue diamond shield is found in the centre of the Bavarian coat of arms.

THE HISTORY OF THE BLUE AND WHITE DIAMONDS

The white and blue diamonds, or rhombuses, in the middle of the Bayern logo are today effectively the Bavarian emblem. The shield of diamonds was the emblem of the Earls of Bogen. It is presumed that many knights once reinforced their shields with an iron grid. From this grid the diamond pattern is to have developed. In a manner of speaking, the Bayern players now also carry a knight's shield on their chest. Perhaps that's why they always feel certain that no opponent can harm them?

the 1993/94 season, 'Bazi' (Bavarian dialect for 'rascal') came Bayern's mascot (right, with Lothar Matthäus). Today, e mascot is a bear and answers to the name of 'Berni'. Here he n be seen arm in arm with Ribéry.

The main stand at the Leopoldstrasse ground.

GRÜNWALDER STADIUM

In September 1926, the Grünwalder Stadium was opened in the Giesing district. Situated at the Grünwalder Strasse road, it held 40,000 and was the first proper stadium in which Bayern reported for duty. But they were only guests there. For a long time, the Grünwalder Stadium was owned by local rivals 1860 until the City of Munich bought it in 1937. Still, for people who lived in Munich it would always remain '1860's ground'. It is actually astonishing to think that Bayern began their success story in someone else's stadium.

FORMER GROUNDS

The pitch on Schyrenstrasse in the meadowland surrounding the river Isar was the site of FC Bayern's first training games. In the founding year of 1900 the club held its first competitive game on the famous area of land known as Theresienwiese, where since 1810 the famous Oktoberfest beer festival is held. FC Bayern's first official football ground was finally built in Clemensstrasse in Munich's Schwabing district, where Bayern played their home games from May 1901 to May 1907. The move to Leopoldstrasse followed in September 1907, where the ground of another club was located – Munich SC, with whom FC Bayern had temporarily merged. Later temporary homes were the MTV ground in Marbachstrasse (1922) and the Teutonia ground at Oberwiesenfeld (1923–25).

SAVE IT FOR 1860

FC Bayern did not always have it easy at the Grünwalder Stadium. Franz Beckenbauer: 'We were just guests there. One of our last second-division games was moved to the Dante Stadium at short notice, because it had suddenly occurred to someone that the pitch had better be saved for 1860.' The Dante Stadium had already been the venue for FC Bayern's games in the last years of World War II.

FC Bayern celebrated many a victory at the Grünwalder Stadium (above and below).

THE OLYMPIC STADIUM

On 28 June 1972, Bayern played their first home game in the Olympic Stadium, so called as it had been constructed for the 1972 Olympic Games. The stadium roof, which was similar to a tent, was particularly impressive. The 5-1 win against Schalke was watched by 80,000 fans and gave the club its first revenue over one million (1.2m German Marks). The Olympic Stadium had come just at the right time. The originally inexpensive team led by Beckenbauer, Maier and Müller was earning more and more money thanks to their successes. Because the bigger ground meant bigger revenue, the club now had the money to keep the team together. The Olympic Stadium could hold twice as many fans as the Grünwalder Stadium. This gave FC Bayern a financial advantage over their competitors, many of whom still had to play in old stadiums. This advantage, however, did not last

for ever. In the 1990s, when almost all the other Bundesliga clubs were playing in new, modern stadiums, Bayern was still based in the Olympic Stadium, which now no longer met the increased demands of the spectators: the tented roof did not offer enough protection from the weather, and it was cold, damp and windy. It was not until April 1999 that the decision was made to build a new arena in Fröttmaning. The 6-3 win against Nuremberg on the penultimate day of the 2004/05 Bundesliga season was the 792nd and last game Bayern played at the Olympic Stadium.

The spectators often seemed lost in the massive orbit of the Olympic Stadium. The running track around the pitch made the ground too spacious, which in turn was bad for the atmosphere.

The Olympic Stadium was considered a particularly beautiful ground when it was constructed.

THE ALLIANZ ARENA

The Beginning

The actual history of the Allianz Arena began in the autumn of 2001. At that time, the citizens of Munich voted with a large majority for a new stadium in the north of Munich (in the Fröttmaning district). The stadium was to cost 340m Euros (£207m at the time) and be financed by FC Bayern and 1860 Munich. At the end of May 2005, the arena, which after refurbishments now offers seating for almost 71,000 spectators, was completed. The opening game was the 201st Munich derby against 1860 on 2 June 2005, which Bayern unexpectedly lost 1-0. On 9 June 2006, the Allianz Arena was the venue for the opening game of the 2006 World Cup (Germany vs. Costa Rica 4-2).

The Arena's Architecture

Particularly striking is the stadium's outer shell made of 2,760 cushions of air, which can be illuminated in white, red and blue. Inside, three steep tiers almost reach down to the edge of the pitch and offer a great view from every seat. The Allianz Arena also offers something to while away the time before and after the game, for instance a huge FC Bayern Munich merchandise shop and the children's Lego World. Particularly worth seeing is the FC Bayern Erlebniswelt (Adventure World), the museum of the Club, recently opened on level 3. In addition kiosks and restaurants en-

tice with a wide range of fare. Not all areas, however, are accessible to everyone. The important people with deep wallets are found in VIP boxes and super restaurants regular ticket holders can't get into. For the less wealthy fans there are particularly cheap standing-room tickets available for the Bayern stand. A season ticket there costs 120 Euros (£96), just 7 Euros (£5.6) per game.

SÄBENER STRASSE TRAINING GROUND

Bayern's training ground on Säbener Strasse is situated in a good neighbourhood in Harlaching. Back in the mid-1960s, Franz Beckenbauer had to get dressed in a wooden hut here, but then the present, 80,000-square-metre train-

ing complex and administrative building was built in 1970. At the time it cost 3.9m German Marks (then £500,000). In 1989 it was renovated and extended, in 2008 it was developed into a super-modern centre of excellence. There are several grass pitches (one with under-soil heating), an artificial pitch and a multipurpose gym available.

Seating plan of the Allianz Arena. The different colours denote the different price categories. They also show where the seats (light orange) and the VIP boxes (grey) are.

The Allianz Arena offers great views of the pitch from every tier.

There are Bayern fans all over the world. The African fan club Kampala (in Uganda) takes to the field in Bayern kits.

The former Bayern goalkeeper Raimond Aumann is the club's main supporter liaison officer. He and his colleagues take care of all fans' enquiries and try to fulfil their wishes.

MILLIONS OF BAYERN FANS

In 2013, FC Bayern had approximately 200,000 club members and more than 3,200 fan clubs with around 240,000 fan-club members. The number of Bayern fans who are not registered as members somewhere is estimated at around 20 million. Only a few top international clubs, such as Real Madrid, FC Barcelona or Manchester United, have more supporters. In the Bundesliga, however, Bayern is head and shoulders above the rest. A distinctive feature of the Bayern fans is that most of them do not live in Munich and its surroundings, but all over Bavaria and indeed across the whole of Germany. No other Bundesliga club has so many fans over such a large area. In the Ruhr district alone there are more than one hundred Bayern fan clubs. And there are even Bayern fans outside of Germany. For this reason the club's website can be accessed not only in German, but also in English, Japanese and Chinese. So that even members of Bayern's Chinese fan club in Shanghai, for example, can learn about what is happening at the club.

TELEVISION, TRIUMPHS AND FANS

FC Bayern would definitely not have as many fans if there was no television. Bayern was the first team whose European Cup games in the 1970s were shown in their entirety on television. Back then, they won the European Cup three consecutive times. This brought the club many new fans in Germany, and that's how the Munich-based club FC Bayern became a club for all Germans. Since Bayern continued to have success, the number of Bayern fans grew more and more. After all, Bayern fans have a much bigger chance of celebrating victories than the fans of other German clubs.

Whenever Bayern win a trophy, thousands of fans celebrate on Munich's central square Marienplatz.

SÜDKURVE · HERZ UND SEELE UNSERE

THE FANS AND THE ATMOSPHERE

The Allianz Arena is practically always sold out, yet it's usually somewhat quieter in the stadium than at other grounds. Fans contributing to the atmosphere are only to be found in the standing area in the south stand, plus some in the north stand. The spectators in the seating areas, on the other hand, normally remain quiet. That is why the Bayern fans on the terrace are demanding a larger standing area in the south stand to improve the atmosphere and the support. Uli Hoeness sees it differently: 'You're responsible for the crap atmosphere and not us,' he told the fans. But perhaps the atmosphere will become better when lots of young new Bayern fans cheer their stars on the pitch at full volume. The fan club Saalachtal could be the role model: at the end of August 2009, 35 children (and five adults) travelled by bus to the Allianz Arena to see Bayern play Werder Bremen. The rather pedestrian 1-1 draw could not spoil the good mood. Even on their return journey the young fans didn't stop singing football chants.

Willy Astor, the man who wrote 'Stern des Südens', often performs his song in person.

Club anthem...

The official club anthem is 'Stern des Südens' (Star of the South), written by Willy Astor and sung by Claus Lessmann, the singer of the hard-rock band Bonfire. It roughly translates as:

'Which Munich football team is known by everyone the world over?
What is the name of this club that holds all the records?
Who has already won everything there is?
Who has kept our Bundesliga going for decades?
FC Bayern, star of the south,
you will never be destroyed,
for we stand side by side in good times and in bad.
FC Bayern, German champions,
yes, that is what my club is called,
yes, that's what it was, and that's what it is and that's what it will always be!'

Previously, 'Forever Number One' had been the club anthem for years.
The fans are also fond of singing the song 'Mir san die Bayern' (We are Bayern).

MUNICH RIVALS

On matchday 28 of the 1966/67 season, Bayern lost 5-2 in Braunschweig. Many observers thought that the players had not really pushed themselves. The fact is: if Bayern had won, that year's league title would not have been lifted by Braunschweig but by Bayern's local rivals 1860. And nobody in the 'red' camp would have wanted the Blues to win the Bundesliga, particularly because 1860 had already won the league in 1966. By the same token, the 'Lions' (as 1860 are nicknamed) were always happy whenever Bayern slipped up. Things would get extra heated when the two rivals faced each other on the field of play.

THE DERBY AGAINST THE 'LIONS'

A game between two clubs from the same city is called a derby. The derby between FC Bayern and 1860 Munich is one of the oldest in Germany. Its history began at the beginning of the last century. In the 1920s, the derbies between the two clubs were the highlight of each season. The crowds flocked to watch and were more excited about this match than about any other game. Sometimes the 'Reds' were number one in Munich, sometimes the 'Blues'. Until the 1960s, Bayern and 1860 were on an equal footing. But then Bayern became the best club not only in Munich but also in the whole of Germany. The 'Lions', on the other hand, did not spend a single season in the Bundesliga between 1981 and 1994. Then they enjoyed ten years in the top flight, before they

were relegated in 2004 (they have been playing second-division football since). To see really competitive Munich derbies, you have to go and watch the two clubs' reserve teams play each other in the Bavarian Regionalliga (the fourth division).

The derby on 14 August 1965: 1860's Timo Konietzka celebrates after scoring the only goal of the game in the first Munich derby played in the Bundesliga.

Derby results

Between 1902 and 2008 there were 204 matches between FC Bayern and 1860. Bayern have won 105 games, drawn 50 and lost 49. They have scored 437 goals to 1860's 278. In the Bundesliga there were 21 victories, 7 draws and 8 defeats. The highest-scoring Bundesliga derby took place on 10 May 1980. In Bayern's 6-1 win, Breitner (2), Karl-Heinz Rummenigge (2), Janzon and Niedermayer got on the scoreboard.

IS THE DERBY A 'CLASS WAR'?

Whenever Bayern play against 1860, many people speak of a 'class war'. By this they mean that the newly rich 'Bigwigs' (FC Bayern) are competing against the genuine 'workers' (1860). But that is not completely correct, of course. In both camps, there are fans who have a lot of money and those who have very little. What is correct, however, is that the 'Blues' have more supporters within Munich itself – at least in relation to the total number of fans. Most Bayern fans travel to the home games from outside the city.

Deserters

Over the decades there have been several players who, despite the rivalry between the clubs, moved from one to the other. 'Deserters' from FC Bayern to 1860 include Peter Grosser (FCB 1960–63, 1860 1963–69), Jupp Kapellmann (FCB 1973–79, 1860 1979–81) and Manfred Schwabl (FCB 1984–86/1989–93, 1860 1994–97). The reverse route, from the 'Blues' to the 'Reds', was taken by Ludwig Kögl (1860 1983–84, FCB 1984–90), Jens Jeremies (1860 1995–98, FCB 1998–2006) and Andreas Görlitz (1860 2001–04, FCB 2004-10).

A legendary 'slap in the face'

Franz Beckenbauer learned the game at Munich SC. In 1958, when he was 13 years old, he planned to join 1860. However, during a game with MSC, he had an encounter with an 1860 player who slapped him. The future 'Kaiser' became so angry he decided to join FC Bayern instead.

The 'Lions' did not have a chance against Mehmet Scholl on 15 February 2003: he contributed three goals to Bayern's 5-0 victory. Scholl is also the best Bayern goalscorer in the history of the derby. He has scored seven goals against the 'Lions', one more than Gerd Müller.

The Allianz Arena is not just the stadium of the 'Reds' but also of the 'Blues'. It is illuminated blue for 1860's games and red for Bayern's games.

President Kurt Landauer

BAYERN'S BEST PRESIDENTS

Many men have been at Bayern's helm, but two stand out: Kurt Landauer, who built the club in the early years, and Wilhelm Neudecker, who oversaw the first successful era in the 1960s.

Kurt Landauer (born 1884), the son of a Jewish businessman and a Bayern member since 1901, was president for the first time in 1913/14. In 1919 he took over office again and held down the post of president, with a small break, for nearly 14 years. Landauer supported the youth set-up and saw to it that the first-team players earned good money. He forbade gadding about and smoking under the threat of severe punishment. It obviously worked: in 1932 Bayern became German champions for the first time. In March 1933, due to the new political situation, Landauer had to step down and emigrate to Switzerland. After his return he was reappointed club president in 1947 and led Bayern until 1951. Kurt Landauer died on 21 December 1961 at the age of 77.

The stern **Wilhelm Neudecker** (born 1913), who had worked his way up from being a bricklayer to a rich building contractor, took over Bayern's presidency in 1962. Neudecker initially renounced spending money on stars, preferring instead to focus on homegrown players. When men like Maier, Beckenbauer and Müller became internationals and commanded bigger wages, the president did everything he could to keep them at FC Bayern. Neudecker was a pig-headed autocrat. That is why he stepped down in 1970 when the players protested against the signing of coach Max Merkel. Wilhelm Neudecker died of heart failure on Christmas Eve 1993.

Neudecker's successors as presidents were **Willi O. Hoffmann** (1979–1985), Professor Dr **Fritz Scherer** (1985–1994) and the most famous man in German football – **Franz Beckenbauer** (1994–2009). The former Bayern business manager **Uli Hoeness** was elected president of FC Bayern in November 2009, at the same time Franz Beckenbauer was named honorary president.

President Neudecker with Gerd Müller.

Left: Chairman Rummenigge, president Hoeness and honorary president Beckenbauer pose in 2001 for an advertisement in wigs and old kits.

Right: Manager Robert Schwan.

THE 'DECISION MAKERS' OF THE MODERN FC BAYERN

Former insurance company director Dr **Robert Schwan** 'invented' modern football management in Germany. Schwan was not only FC Bayern's business manager but also Franz Beckenbauer's agent. His last act for FC Bayern was selling the 'Kaiser' to Cosmos New York in 1977. Schwan's successor in 1979 was the former Bayern player **Uli Hoeness**. As 'Mr Bayern' the business manager became a legend. In order to be successful, he felt, a business manager needed to have been a first-class player himself. He also should be financially independent and always faithful to his club. As a player, Hoeness had won all possible titles. He had also earned millions with non-footballing deals (above all with a sausage factory specialising in German bratwurst) and had always been a true Bayern man. So it comes as no surprise that under Hoeness, FC Bayern became the most successful and wealthiest club in Germany. Next to Hoeness, the most important man at Bayern is former Bayern striker **Karl-Heinz Rummenigge**, now the chairman. Hoeness's successor is **Matthias Sammer** (carrying the title Director of Sports), now the person to take care of pithy one-liners and admonitory speeches.

LEDERHOSEN

During the 1979/80 season Bayern president Willi O. Hoffmann together with Uli Hoeness and Paul Breitner developed the idea of giving the Bayern players lederhosen (the leather work shorts traditionally worn in the Alpine regions). At the time, rival fans had taken up singing 'Pull down Bayern's lederhosen' (to the tune of 'Yellow Submarine' by The Beatles). The idea was to turn a derogatory chant upon itself and say: look, we're indeed wearing lederhosen – but no one is pulling them off us! Lederhosen have since become a Bayern trademark. All new signings receive a pair and have to wear them for the traditional visit to the Oktoberfest.

Gomez and Schweinsteiger in lederhosen.

Bayern is not just by far and away the best German football club; the players, of course, are also the best and have set the most records. But not all the records are glorious ...

THE TOP STRIKERS

The ranking of the best Bundesliga strikers of FC Bayern (until end of 2012/13 season): 1st Gerd Müller 0.85 goals per game (427 matches / 365 goals); 2nd Mario Gomez 0.68 (94 / 64); 3rd Luca Toni 0.63 (60 / 38); 4th Mario Mandzukić 0.62 (24/15); 5th Roy Makaay 0.6 (129 / 78); 6th Arjen Robben 0.65 (62 / 40); 7th Giovane Elber 0.54 (169 / 92); 8th Karl-Heinz Rummenigge 0.52 (310 / 162).

THE FLOP STRIKERS

Bayern's history is full of strikers who cost millions but didn't really score. A few examples: 1988 Ekström (2.3m German Marks – 7 goals in 23 matches, average 0.33); 1989 Mihajlovic (1.9m – 4 in 34, average 0.25), 1989 McInally (10 in 40, average 0.25); 1991 Mazinho (2m – 11 in 49, average 0.22); 1994 Papin (6m – 3 in 27, average 0.11); 1994 Kostadinov (1.1m – 7 in 27, average 0.25).

MÜLLER'S RECORDS

The incomparable Gerd Müller (566 goals from 607 official matches for FC Bayern) was not only the best and most efficient Bundesliga goalscorer of all time, he also held other records: he was a seven-time Golden Boot winner (1967/69/70/72/73/74/78), he scored the most goals in one season (40 in 1971/72) and he had the longest scoring run (16 consecutive games with at least one goal from 27 September 1969 to 3 March 1970). In addition he scored seven hat-tricks under the German definition (three goals without reply in one half). Further records: 78 goals from 62 domestic cup games and 66 goals from 74 European games.

THE FASTEST BUNDESLIGA GOALSCORER ...

is Giovane Elber. On 31 January 1998 he needed just 11 seconds to put the ball into Hamburg's net.

PENALTY KING

Gerd Müller has taken the most penalties (63) – and has also missed the most (12 times). His goal probability was 80.95 per cent and hence well above the average of 75 per cent. Manfred Kaltz from Hamburg was even better: he converted 56 out of 60 penalties (93.33 per cent). Paul Breitner (1980/81) converted the most penalties in one season, with nine.

KAHN'S RECORDS

Oliver Kahn won more games than any other Bundesliga player (310 in 557 matches). He is the goalkeeper with the most clean sheets in all (197) and also the one who conceded the fewest goals and had the most clean sheets in a single season (21 goals conceded in 2007/08, 19 clean sheets in 2001/02). The record for longest period without conceding a goal does not belong to Kahn, though. In the Bundesliga

Top goalscorer Gerd Müller in action.

he kept a clean sheet for 803 minutes, but Timo Hildebrand once managed 884 minutes. Bayern's club record (across all competitions) has been held since 2011/12 by Manuel Neuer who went 1,147 minutes unbeaten. Kahn lasted just 1,013 minutes.

THE RECORD FOR MOST CONSECUTIVE APPEARANCES ...

is held by Sepp Maier (442 matches).

THE FASTEST GOAL IN THE CHAMPIONS LEAGUE ...

was scored by Roy Makaay. On 7 March 2007 he needed just 10 seconds to score against Real Madrid.

THE MOST SUCCESSFUL SUPER SUB OF THE BUNDESLIGA ...

is still Alexander Zickler. He scored 18 goals after being brought into the game. Second place: Mehmet Scholl with 14 goals.

MOST OFTEN BROUGHT INTO THE GAME ...

was Mehmet Scholl (123 times). As regards being taken off, he is in sixth place (114 times).

THE MOST LEAGUE TITLES ...

have been won by Oliver Kahn and Mehmet Scholl. Both players won the Bundesliga eight times with Bayern Munich. Klaus Augenthaler, Lothar Matthäus and Alexander Zickler, who also collected all German league titles at FC Bayern, each have won the Bundesliga seven times. Seven titles were also won by the substitute goalkeeper Bernd Dreher – even though he made only 13 league appearances in eleven years!

Record goalkeeper Oliver Kahn.

THE MOST GERMAN CUPS ...

were won by Oliver Kahn: six trophies from seven finals.

THE MOST BOOKINGS OF ALL BUNDESLIGA PLAYERS ...

were collected by Stefan Effenberg: he saw the yellow card 111 times (!) with Bayern and Mönchengladbach. The former Leverkusen player Jens Nowotny has been sent off most often (five red cards, three second yellows). The Bayern player Samuel Kuffour is just behind him: four red cards and three second yellows.

RECORD HONOURS

Bayern players were voted German Footballer of the Year 18 times (Beckenbauer four times, Maier three times, Müller, Kahn and Ballack twice each, Karl-Heinz Rummenigge, Breitner, Matthäus, Robben and Schweinsteiger once each). Bayern players have in addition been voted European Footballer of the Year five times (Beckenbauer twice, Rummenigge twice and Müller once).

THE MOST BUNDESLIGA WINS IN A ROW...

went to Willy Sagnol and Lúcio (each 15), followed by another eight (!) Bayern players, each with 13 wins in a row.

THE MOST GOALS IN THE SHORTEST TIME ...

were scored by Dieter Hoeness. On 25 February 1984 he scored five goals between the 67th and 89th minute against Eintracht Frankfurt.

BAYERN PLAYERS IN THE NATIONAL TEAM

The first Bayern international was the right winger Max Gablonsky. He was called up to the national team after a good showing in the Southern German Championship (Bayern finished as runners-up) for the game against Belgium on 16 May 1910 in Duisburg. It was an extraordinary game. The final of the national championship between Karlsruher FV and Holstein Kiel had taken place the day before, which meant the best players were missing. Only seven players arrived in Duisburg, so the national team had to be supplemented by reserves. Even the fast Gablonsky could do nothing – Belgium won 3-0. Since then Bayern has sent a further 83 players onto the pitch for international games. Those 84 Bayern internationals have won a total of 1,889 caps (as of 2 June 2013). FC Bayern leads all other German clubs both as concerns the number of internationals (second place goes to Hamburg with 50) and appearances made (Cologne in second place has 793).

BAYERN'S WORLD CUP WINNERS

Until 2010, Bayern players had been called up to a World Cup squad 58 times. Six Bayern players were on the pitch for West Germany in the 1974 final (2-1 against the Netherlands): **Maier** – Vogts, **Breitner** – **Schwarzenbeck**, **Beckenbauer**, Bonhof – Grabowski, **Uli Hoeness**, **Gerd Müller**.

In 1990 (when the final was won 1-0 against Argentina), there were five Bayern players in the World Cup squad (Augenthaler, Kohler, Pflügler, Reuter, Aumann) and five former or future Bayern players (Berthold, Brehme, Klinsmann, Matthäus, Thon).

Seven Bayern players made the 2010 World Cup squad and finished 3rd: Hans Jörg Butt, Holger Badstuber, Philipp Lahm, Bastian Schweinsteiger, Mario Gomez, Miroslav Klose, Thomas Müller.

2010 World Cup, against England in the round of 16: two-time goalscorer Thomas Müller (left) celebrates Germany's 4-1 win with Bastian Schweinsteiger.

Former Bayern player Franz Beckenbauer (2nd from left) leads the West German national team to the World Cup title in 1990. To his left are the then-Bayern players Klaus Augenthaler and Stefan Reuter as well as the future Bayern player and coach Jürgen Klinsmann.

BAYERN'S GERMAN INTERNATIONALS

Franz Beckenbauer 103, WC, EC
Lothar Matthäus 96 (150), WC, EC
Sepp Maier 95, WC, EC
Oliver Kahn 86
Karl-Heinz Rummenigge 78 (95), EC
Gerd Müller 62, WC, EC
Thomas Helmer 58 (68), EC
Markus Babbel 51, EC
Jens Jeremies 47 (55)
Paul Breitner 46 (48), WC, EC
Georg Schwarzenbeck 44, WC, EC
Michael Ballack 41 (98)
Thomas Linke 41 (43)
Ludwig Goldbrunner 39
Mehmet Scholl 36, EC
Uli Hoeness 35, WC, EC
Christian Ziege 31 (72), EC
Carsten Jancker 29 (33)
Jürgen Klinsmann 23 (108), WC, EC
Thomas Strunz 21 (41), EC
Klaus Augenthaler 27, WC
Wolfgang Dremmler 27
Stefan Reuter 18 (69), WC, EC
Ludwig Hofmann 18
Sebastian Deisler 17 (36)
Stefan Effenberg 14 (35)
Michael Tarnat 15 (19)
Jakob Streitle 15
Josef Pöttinger 14
Torsten Frings 13 (79)
Jürgen Kohler 12 (105), WC, EC
Andreas Brehme 12 (86), WC
Dietmar Hamann 12 (59)
Olaf Thon 12 (52), WC
Alexander Zickler 12
Mario Basler 11 (30)

Sigmund Haringer 11 (15)
Willi Giesemann 11 (14)
Hans Pflügler 11, WC
Norbert Eder 9
Conrad Heidkamp 8 (9)
Josef Bergmaier 8
Emil Kutterer 8
Wilhelm Simetsreiter 8
Hans Dorfner 7
Hans Bauer 5, WC
Dieter Hoeness 4 (6)
Gerhard Siedl 4 (6)
Raimond Aumann 4
Max Gablonsky 4
Oskar Rohr 4
Franz Roth 4
Karl Mai 3 (21), WC
Jupp Kapellmann 3 (5)
Georg Schneider 3
Tobias Rau 2 (7)
Andreas Görlitz 2
Ludwig Kögl 2
Franz Krumm 2
Michael Rummenigge 2
Roland Wohlfarth 2
Herbert Erhardt 1 (50), WC
Hans Jörg Butt 1 (4)
Ludwig Hofmeister 1 (2)
Bruno Labbadia 1 (2)
Dieter Brenninger 1
Fritz Fürst 1
Rudolf Nafziger 1
Ernst Nagelschmitz 1
Kurt Niedermayer 1
Rainer Ohlhauser 1
Werner Olk 1, Hans Welker 1

Currently active players:
(as of 2 June 2013)

Bastian Schweinsteiger 98
Philipp Lahm 83 (98)
Miroslav Klose 43 (127)
Thomas Müller 41
Lukas Podolski 32 (110)
Mario Gomez 33 (58)
Toni Kroos 31 (35)
Holger Badstuber 30
Manuel Neuer 18 (38)
Jérôme Boateng 16 (29)
Marcell Jansen 12 (39)

There are six Bayern players among the top nine goalscorers in the history of the national team (all goals for all clubs up until 2 June 2013):

Gerd Müller 68
Miroslav Klose 67
Jürgen Klinsmann 47
(Rudi Völler 47)
Karl-Heinz Rummenigge 45
(Uwe Seeler 43)
Michael Ballack 42
(Oliver Bierhoff 37)
Lukas Podolski 44

World-class goalkeeper: Manuel Neuer.

In 2007, they were still playing for Bayern's Under-19 team (here in the final for the national championships), today they are first-team regulars: Thomas Müller and Holger Badstuber.

The FC Bayern youth academy.

YOUTH AND TALENT

Youth and success are not mutually exclusive. When Bayern was promoted to the Bundesliga in 1964/65, the average age of their players was just 21.8 years. Of the 25 players who wore the Bayern shirt, 14 were homegrown. Time and again fresh young talent has come up through the ranks. In 2012/13, seven players who had been schooled at the club were in the first-team squad. The best-known of them are now Germany regulars (Philipp Lahm, Bastian Schweinsteiger, Holger Badstuber, Thomas Müller).

> **The biggest triumphs of the reserves**
> (formerly lnown as Bayern Amateurs)
> National amateur championship finalists in 1983 and 1987
> Regionalliga South (then part of the multi-tiered third division) champions in 2004
> Quarter-finalists of the 1994/95 and 2004/05 DFB-Pokal

JUNIOR TEAM

In 1995 FC Bayern reformed their youth program and created the 'junior team'. It consists of the reserves, who compete in the fourth division, as well as eleven youth teams (from the Under-8s to the Under-19s), which are coached by 26 instructors. The older players (the Under-19s and Under-17s) almost work under professional conditions, having six training sessions per week. For the most talented players from outside Munich, there is a boarding house with 13 single rooms at the Säbener Strasse training grounds.

DIAMOND EYE …

is the nickname of 'Tiger' Hermann Gerland. Since 1990, as a reserve- and youth-team coach, he's gained a reputation for recognising talent early and being able to successfully foster it. Gerland has worked with many players who would later become famous – for example Dietmar Hamann, Christian Nerlinger, Sammy Kuffour, Markus Babbel, Bastian Schweinsteiger and Philipp Lahm. He also helped Thomas Müller and Holger Badstuber into the first team. But not every talent immediately broke into the senior side. Bayern often loaned out young players (such as Toni Kroos to Leverkusen or David Alaba to Hoffenheim) if they needed time to mature. Toni Kroos made the World Cup squad after his return to Munich in 2010, while David Alaba is now a regular starting player for Bayern and the Austrian national team.

THE ONLY TRUE BAVARIANS

On 10 February 2010, Diego Armando Contento – named after the famous Maradona – made his professional Bayern debut during a 6-2 win against SpVgg Greuther Fürth in the German cup. The defender was only the second player since 1965 who had spent his entire career until that point with FC Bayern. The first to climb up through every Bayern youth team was Max Eberl, currently business manager of Borussia Mönchengladbach. Eberl even won the national Under-17 championship with Bayern in 1989, though he later made only one Bundesliga appearance for his hometown club. If Contento, who joined Bayern as a five-year-old in 1995, manages to break into the first team, he will be a huge exception as all the great Bayern players have begun their careers elsewhere: Beckenbauer (Munich SC), Gerd Müller (TSV Nördlingen), Thomas Müller (TSV Pähl), Maier (TSV Haar), Lahm (TV Gern Munich) and Schweinsteiger (TSV Rosenheim).

One-club man Diego Contento.

National youth championships
There are national championships in youth football since 1969 in Germany. So far, Bayern have won the Under-19 title three times and the Under-17 championship four times. At both levels, VfB Stuttgart are the record title holders (ten and six titles respectively).

'Diamond Eye' Hermann Gerland, here with Bastian Schweinsteiger, long-time coach of the Bayern reserves and assistant coach of the Bundesliga team.

Women's football in England in 1895.

A Long Road To Recognition

The first women's football teams were formed in England even before 1900. However, the resistance of men against women who ran around publicly in shorts prevented the rapid spread of women's football. When a few decades later the first women appeared on football pitches in Germany the reaction was no different. The German FA (DFB) forbade its clubs to create women's football divisions or to make grounds available for women's teams. Yet women's football was becoming more and more popular, and in 1970 the DFB had to allow women to play the game. In the same year FC Bayern's women's football division was formed. Today German women's football is universally respected and successful. The German women's national team has won two World Cups and eight European Championships. Bayern Ladies have also made a name for themselves.

The 1976 Championship And 2012 Cup Victory

FC Bayern is one of only two German clubs that have won national championships in both men's and women's football. While the men have collected one title after the other, the women have succeeded only once despite making four appearances in finals. In the 1976 final they won the German championship by defeating Tennis Borussia Berlin 4-2 after extra time.

A massive celebration! The Bayern ladies win the 2012 DFB-Pokal!

The Bayern ladies play at Aschenheim Sports Park.
The stadium can hold 3,000 spectators.

FC Bayern is also the only club that has reached German cup finals in the men's game and women's football at the same time. While the men missed out on winning their 16th cup in Berlin against Dortmund in 2012, the women had more success a few hours earlier in Cologne. In their third appearance in a final, after 1988 and 1990, they lifted the cup against a strong FFC Frankfurt team which was studded with internationals! In the 63rd minute Sarah Hagen headed home from a corner taken by Katharina Baunach to bring Bayern ahead. In the final minute Ivana Rudelic hit Frankfurt on the break and made it 2-0.

DOING WELL IN THE BUNDESLIGA

Despite the 1976 national title and a string of Bavarian trophies during the early years of women's football in Germany (19 Bavarian championships in a row!), the cup victory of 2012 is surely the greatest success of Bayern's women's team. After a brief stay out of the top flight, they are now also one of the best teams in the women's Bundesliga (formed in 1990). In the 2008/09 season, Bayern lost out on first place by only one goal and qualified as runners-up for the Women's Champions League for the first time. There they reached the round of 16. In 2012/13 they finished in fourth

place in the Bundesliga, but beat the top teams Potsdam and Frankfurt as well as new champions Wolfsburg at home.

WELL-KNOWN PLAYERS

The best-known member of the 1976 championship-winning team was the international (56 caps) and later coach **Sissy Raith**. Germany goalkeeper **Nadine Angerer** stood between the sticks for Bayern for two seasons from 1999 to 2001, before she moved to Potsdam. **Simone Laudehr**, who scored the deciding second goal in the 2007 World Cup final against Brazil, spent one season (2003/04) at FC Bayern. An international with a powerful shot, **Melanie Behringer** wore the FC Bayern colours for two years (2008–10). Forward **Petra Wimbersky**, World Cup winner and European Champion, had two stints at Bayern (1999–2002 and 2010–12). The 2012/13 Bundesliga squad had a strong American bent. New signing **Gina Lewandowski** joined from FFC Frankfurt and the two German-Americans **Niki Cross** and **Rebecca Huyleur** were mainstays in defence; also from the USA are **Amber Brooks** and **Sarah Hagen**. The best known player of the squad certainly is the Germany international **Lena Lotzen**. At Euro 2013 in Sweden the midfielder was a regular and returned to Munich as a European Champion. A talented hopeful in attack is the Under-19 international **Sarah Romert**.

LIST OF BAYERN COACHES SINCE 1963

Beckenbauer, Franz (*11.9.1945). The 'Kaiser' already had a few coaching jobs behind him (Olympique Marseille, World Cup winner with the national team in 1990) when he came to the rescue at Bayern. Twice (1994 and 1996) he took over the team towards the end of the season and twice he won a title (league championship, UEFA Cup).

Cajkovski, Zlatko (*24.11.1923†27.7.1998). In 1963 Bayern, who at the time were in the 2nd division, signed the small, stout and jolly Yugoslavian Zlatko 'Čik' Cajkovski as coach, a year after he had led FC Cologne to the German championship. Under the direction of the former world-class player, who could hardly speak a word of German ('I'm not a German teacher, but a football teacher'), the comet-like rise of the club began: 1965 promotion to the Bundesliga, 1966 and 1967 German cup winners, 1967 winners of the Cup Winner's Cup.

Cramer, Dettmar (*4.4.1925). Under Dettmar Cramer, FC Bayern enjoyed success only on the international stage, winning the European Cup in 1975 and 1976 and then the Intercontinental Cup. For many experts, the clever 'professor of football' was the 'great theorist' among coaches. Before and after his time in Munich, Cramer travelled to countless countries as a coach.

Csernai, Pal (*21.10.1932). Known as the 'man with the silk cravat' and inventor of the 'PAL system' (meaning zonal defending, which at that time was highly unusual), Gyula Lorant's former assistant made Bundesliga history. His successes: 1980 and 1981 league champion, 1983 DFB-Pokal winner, 1982 European Cup finalist.

Guardiola, Josep (*18.1.1971)
The excellent midfielder's biggest triumph was winning the 1992 European Cup with FC Barcelona under coach Johan Cruyff. Between 2008 and 2012, as a coach, he made Barça the best team in Europe. A short passing game and aggressive pressing were the hallmarks of a team that won 14 out of a possible 19 titles during this time, two of which came in the biggest competition, the Champions League. After a year off in New York, he took over at Bayern on 1 July 2013 and hopes to achieve similar success in Munich.

Stepped down with the treble in 2013: Jupp Heynckes.

Heynckes, Jupp (*9.5.1945). In 1987, Uli Hoeness made Jupp Heynckes the successor to Udo Lattek. Before that, Heynckes had been successful as both player and coach with Borussia Mönchengladbach. He did well domestically (winning the Bundesliga twice, finishing second twice) but failed three times in a row in the semi-finals of the European cup competitions between 1989 and 1991. When things went even further downhill during the 1991/92 season, his friend Uli Hoeness sacked him with a heavy heart. In 2009 he had a brief stay in Munich to replace the fired Jürgen Klinsmann. Heynckes was back again in the 2011/12 season to lead FCB to new successes as an 'old-school' coach. After 23 years, Jupp Heynckes won the league once again in 2013. It was his third Bundesliga title after 1989 and 1990 with Bayern Munich. In 2013, he also won his first German cup and then the Champions League, too. (Which he had already won, along with the Intercontinenal Cup, in 1998 as Real Madrid coach.) Last but not least, at 68 years of age he became the oldest coach to lift the Bundesliga title.

Hitzfeld, Ottmar (*12.1.1949). Borussia Dortmund's success coach (a two-time league champion and Champions League winner) replaced Giovanni Trapattoni ahead of the 1998/99 season. Ottmar Hitzfeld managed to tame Bayern, then deemed 'uncoachable', and led them to more trophies than any coach before him: 1999, 2000, 2001, 2003 Bundesliga champion, 2000, 2003 German cup winner, 2001 Champions League winner, 2001 Intercontinental Cup winner. However, when the 2003/04 season yielded no silverware, he was all of a sudden considered 'too soft' in his approach with the pros. Hitzfeld made way for the 'stern' Felix Magath but returned on 31 January 2007. Once more he had success domestically, winning his third double with Bayern in 2008.

Klinsmann, Jürgen (*30.7.1964). Formerly a brilliant striker and Germany manager, Klinsmann started off the 2008/09 season with lots of ideas but failed in practice. Due to his lack of success he was sacked before the season was over.

Lattek, Udo (*16.1.1935). Lattek was a fairly unknown coach with the German FA when he followed Branko Zebec in March 1970. He had to thank Franz Beckenbauer for getting the post, who had got to know and appreciate him as assistant coach to German national manager Helmut Schön. Under Lattek, who could motivate the players well, FC Bayern entered its most successful era. After his first stint at the club (which lasted until 1975), Lattek returned in 1983. Under his guidance, FC Bayern won six league titles (1972–74, 1985–87), three domestic cups (1971, 1984, 1986) and the European Cup (1974).

Magath, Felix (*26.7.1953). The technically gifted former international had already won a reputation for being a particularly stern coach ('Quality comes from pain') at the beginning of his managerial career. The passionate chess player brought order and discipline to Bayern when he joined in 2004. In 2005 and 2006 he won the double twice in a row, the first-ever coach to do so, but he wasn't able to lift trophies in Europe and didn't satisfy the fans' yearning for the beautiful (and not just successful) game.

Rehhagel, Otto (*9.8.1938). Rehhagel had tremendous success with Bayern's long-time rivals Werder Bremen. But he didn't meet expectations as Bayern coach. Despite pithy quips ('Everyone can say what I want') and even though his team was in 2nd place, he was let go before the end of the 1995/96 season. After his departure he won promotion with Kaiserslautern and then led this club to a sensational Bundesliga title; he followed this in 2004 by equally sensationally winning the European Championships as national manager of Greece.

Ribbeck, Erich (*13.6.1937). The experienced Bundesliga coach (his biggest success was winning the UEFA Cup in 1988 with Leverkusen) had already gone into retirement when he was asked to take over at Bayern in March 1992, as the club was in a deep crisis. In December 1993 he was sacked and replaced by Franz Beckenbauer, even though Bayern were in 2nd place. The 'Kaiser' then led the team to the league title. In later years, Ribbeck worked without much success for Leverkusen and as Germany manager.

Trapattoni, Giovanni (*17.3.1939). The Italian gentleman joined Bayern as the most successful coach in the world (17 titles!) in 1994. However, due to language problems he did not get along well at first. After the unfortunate attempt with Otto Rehhagel, Bayern signed him for a second time, and now he delivered a league title. But there was still a lot of criticism, for his team played unattractive schematic football.

Pep Guardiola

Van Gaal, Louis (*8.8.1951). The Dutchman coached Ajax Amsterdam, FC Barcelona and the Dutch national team, among others. His trophy haul is impressive; with Ajax he even won the Champions League in 1995. He nearly managed to pull off this feat with FC Bayern in 2010, but after winning the Bundesliga and the DFB-Pokal, Bayern fell at the final hurdle in the Champions League (losing the final against Inter 2-0). After disappointments in all competitions and many arguments he was let go on 10 April 2011.

Zebec, Branko (*17.5.1929 †26.9.1988). When the Yugoslavian record international joined Bayern in 1968 he did not have much coaching experience. But during the stern man's time at the helm, Bayern won their first Bundesliga title and also the DFB-Pokal. After he was given the boot in Munich, he enjoyed success with Hamburg, where he had a lot of influence on the future Bayern coach Felix Magath.

List of Bayern coaches in chronological order since 1963

Zlatko Čajkovski (1963–68)
Branko Zebec (1968–70)*
Udo Lattek (1970–75)*
Dettmar Cramer (1975–78)*
Gyula Lorant (1978/79)*
Pal Csernai (1979–83)*
Reinhard Saftig (1983)
Udo Lattek (1983–87)
Jupp Heynckes (1987–1991)*
Soren Lerby (1991/92)*
Erich Ribbeck (1992–94)*
Franz Beckenbauer (1994)
Giovanni Trapattoni (1994/95)
Otto Rehhagel (1995/96)*
Franz Beckenbauer (1996)
Giovanni Trapattoni (1996–98)
Ottmar Hitzfeld (1998–2004)
Felix Magath (2004–07)
Ottmar Hitzfeld (2007/08)
Jürgen Klinsmann (2008/09)*
Jupp Heynckes (2009)
Louis van Gaal (2009–2011)*
Jupp Heynckes (2011–13)
Josep Guardiola (since 2013)
*= replaced before the end of the season

Ottmar Hitzfeld bids a tearful farewell after winning the 2008 league title as Bayern coach.

The all-time Bayern XI

On the occasion of the opening match in the Allianz Arena, FC Bayern presented the all-time best Bayern players, as chosen by the fans: Sepp Maier – Klaus Augenthaler, Georg 'Katsche' Schwarzenbeck, Franz Beckenbauer, Paul Breitner – Stefan Effenberg, Lothar Matthäus, Mehmet Scholl – Giovane Elber, Gerd Müller, Karl-Heinz Rummenigge.

Josef Bergmaier

LIST OF BAYERN PLAYERS (SELECTION)

(As of 1 June 2013)

Abbreviations: DFB = German cup winner,
GC = German champion
(includes the pre-Bundesliga title),
CL = Champions League/European Cup winner,
UEFA = UEFA Cup winner,
CWC = Cup Winners' Cup winner,
In brackets: years at Bayern (sometimes intermittently), Bundesliga games/goals, matches in the Oberliga (OL)

A

Alaba, David (*24.6.1992), small Austrian with huge talent (2009–13, 58/5). 2 x GC, 2 x DFB, 1 x CL

Altintop, Hamit (*8.12.1982), Turkish international with lots of fighting spirit (2007–11, 63/7). 2 x GC, 1 x DFB

Andersson, Patrick (*18.8.1971), at times head of the Bayern defence (1999–2001, 38/11). 1 x DFB, 2 x GC, 1 x CL

Augenthaler, Klaus (*26.9.1957), grumpy successor to Beckenbauer as sweeper (1977–91, 404/52). 3 x DFB, 7 x GC

Aumann, Raimond (*12.10.1963), the Jungle Book bear ('Baloo' was his nickname) in goal (1984–94, 216). 6 x GC

B

Babbel, Markus (*8.9.1972), defender, genuine Bavarian and good in the air (1991–99, 154/8). 1 x DFB, 2 x GC, 1 x UEFA

Badstuber, Holger (*13.3.1989), a smart centre back with great abilities (2009–13, 101/1). 2 x GC, 2 x DFB, 1 x CL

Ballack, Michael (*26.9.1976), no midfielder in the world was as free-scoring as he was in his prime (2002–06, 107/44). 3 x DFB, 1 x GC

Basler, Mario (*18.12.1968), free-kick expert and resident lazy genius (1996–2000, 78/18). 1 x DFB, 2 x GC

Bauer, Hans (*28.7.1927), a 'golden boy' at left back (1948–59, OL: 226/3)

Beckenbauer, Franz (*11.9.1945), sweeper and football's 'Kaiser' (1965–77, 396/44). 4 x DFB, 4 x GC, 3 x CL, 1 x CWC

Bender, Manfred (*24.5.1966), midfielder and set-piece specialist (1989–92, 77/9). 1 x GC

Bergmaier, Josef (*5.3.1909 †5.3.1943), right winger who loved to dribble (1929–38). 1 x GC

Boateng, Jérôme (*3.9.1988), Germany defender with Ghanaian father (2009–13, 101/1) 2 x GC, 2 x DFB, 1 x CL

Brehme, Andreas (*9.11.1960), full back with two strong feet (1986–88, 59/7). 1 x GC

Breitner, Paul (*5.9.1951), midfield maestro with a sharp tongue (1970–83, 255/83). 1 x DFB, 5 x GC, 1 x CL

Mario Gomez

Brenninger, Dieter (*16.2.1944), left winger from Alternerding (1962–71, BL: 190/59). 4 x DFB, 1 x GC, 1 x CWC

C

Contento, Diego Armando (*1.5.1990), talented defender with famous first name (2009–13, 39/0). 2 x GC, 2 x DFB, 1 x CL

D

Dante (*18.10.1983), commanding Brazilian centre back with an impressive hairdo (2012/13, 29/1). 1 x GC, 1 x DFB, 1 x CL

Deisler, Sebastian (*5.1.1980), big talent but short career (2002–07, 62/8). 3 x DFB, 3 x GC

Del'Haye, Karl (*18.8.1955), nippy winger who was wasted on the bench (1980–84, 74/7). 2 x DFB, 1 x GC

Demichelis, Martín (*20.12.1980), centre back from Argentina (2003–10, 174/13). 4 x GC, 4 x DFB

Dorfner, Hans (*3.7.1965), orchestrated play for many years (1986–91, 111/16). 3 x GC

Dremmler, Wolfgang (*12.7.1954), Paul Breitner's 'water carrier' (1979–86, 172/6). 3 x DFB, 4 x GC

Dürnberger, Bernd (*17.9.1953), hard-working midfielder (1972–85, 375/38). 2 x DFB, 5 x GC, 3 x CL

E

Eder, Norbert (*7.11.1955), man-marker from Bibergau who took no prisoners (1984–88, 132/6). 1 x DFB, 3 x GC

Effenberg, Stefan (*2.8.1968), was the boss and let everyone know about it (1990–2002, 160/35). 2 x DFB, 3 x GC, 1 x CL

Elber, Giovane (*23.7.1972), Brazilian goalscorer known for his celebrations (1997–2003, 169/92). 3 x DFB, 4 x GC, 1 x CL

F

Fink, Thorsten (*29.10.1967), useful team player in midfield (1997–2003, 149/4). 3 x DFB, 4 x GC, 1 x CL

Flick, Hans-Dieter (*24.2.1965), rather inconspicuous midfielder (1985–90, 104/6). 1 x DFB, 3 x GC

G

Gablonsky, Max (*1.1.1890 †16.7.1969), long-time presence on the right wing (500 goals by 1922)

Giesemann, Willi (*2.9.1937), brilliant defender during the Oberliga days (1959–63, OL: 114/13)

Goldbrunner, Ludwig (*5.3.1908 †26.9.1981), centre half extraordinaire, team captain 1937–1941. 1 x GC

Gomez, Mario (*10.7.1985), most expensive Bayern striker, commanded a 35m Euro transfer fee (2009–13, 115/75). 2 x GC, 2 x DFB, 1 x CL

Ludwig Hofmann

Grahammer, Roland (*3.11.1963), talented full back (1988–93, 102/2). 2 x GC

Grosser, Peter (*28.9.1938), outstandingly skilful player in the pre-Bundesliga era (1958–63, OL: 134/65)

Gustavo, Luiz (*23.7.1987), multi-purpose Brazilian from Pindamonhangaba (2011–13, 64/6). 1 x GC, 1 x DFB, 1 x CL

H

Hamann, Dietmar (*27.8.1973), a long-time regular in right-sided midfield (1993–98, 106/6). 2 x GC, 1 x UEFA

Hansen, Johnny (*14.11.1943), reliable Danish defender (1969–76, 164/7). 1 x DFB, 3 x GC, 3 x CL

Hargreaves, Owen (*20.1.1981), agile British midfielder who covered Effenberg's back (2000–07, 145/5). 3 x GC, 4 x GC, 1 x CL

Haringer, Sigmund (*9.12.1908 †23.2.1975), defender in the 1932 championship team. 1 x GC

Heidkamp, Conrad (*27.9.1905 †6.3.1994), captain of the 1932 championship team. 1 x GC

Helmer, Thomas (*21.4.1965), defender and team captain (1992–99, 191/24). 1x DFB, 3x GC, 1 x UEFA

Hoeness, Dieter (*7.1.1953), strong header of the ball and courageous forward (1979–87, 224/102). 3 x DFB, 5 x GC

Hoeness, Uli (*5.1.1952), fleet-footed, counter-attacking forward (1970–79, 239/86). 1 x DFB, 3 x GC, 3 x CL

Hofmann, Ludwig (*9.6.1900 †2.10.1935), technically strong left winger in the 1920s

Horsmann, Udo (*30.3.1952), unspectacular defender (1975–83, 242/20). 1 x DFB, 2 x GC, 1 x CL

IJ

Jancker, Carsten (*28.8.1974), bald-headed target man (1996–2002, 143/48). 2 x DFB, 4 x GC, 1 x CL

Janzon, Norbert (*21.12.1950), the first of many players to move from Karlsruhe to Bayern (1977–81, 84/20). 2 x GC

Jeremies, Jens (*5.3.1974), dogged holding midfielder (1998–2006, 163/6). 4 x DFB, 6 x GC, 1 x CL

Jorginho (*17.8.1964), full back with ball skills from Brazil (1992–94, 67/5). 1 x GC

Junghans, Walter (*26.10.1958), luckless successor to Sepp Maier (1978–82, 67). 1 x DFB, 2 x GC

K

Kahn, Oliver (*15.6.1969), the world's best goalkeeper was also known for temper tantrums (1994–2008, 429). 6 x DFB, 8 x GC, 1 x CL

Kapellmann, Jupp (*19.12.1949), medical student, fast and smart (1973–79, 165/17). 1 x GC, 3 x CL

Klinsmann, Jürgen (*30.7.1964), Swabian goalscorer, always smiling (1995–97, 65/31). 1 x GC, 1 x CWC

Klose, Miroslav (*9.6.1978), so good in the air that he celebrated goals with somersaults(2007–11, 98/24). 2 x GC, 2 x DFB

Kögl, Ludwig (*7.3.1966), nippy dribbler and firm fan favourite (1984–90, 149/8). 1 x DFB, 5 x GC

Kohler, Jürgen (*6.10.1965), best and once most expensive of Bayern's man-markers (1989–91, 55/6). 1 x GC

Koulmann, Dieter (*4.12.1939), midfielder during the promotion campaign (1965–68, 77/12). 2 x DFB, 1 x CWC

Kovac, Robert (*6.4.1974), ball-winning defender from Croatia (2001–05, 94/0). 2 x DFB, 2 x GC

Kraus, Wolfgang (*20.8.1953), industrious midfielder (1979–84, 138/17). 2 x DFB, 2 x GC

Kreuzer, Oliver (*13.11.1965), a regular at the heart of the defence (1991–97, 282/14). 2 x GC, 1 x UEFA

Kroos, Toni (*4.1.1990), a number 10 player who is comfortable on the ball (2007–13, 101/11). 2 x GC, 2 x DFB, 1 x CL

Krumm, Franz (*16.10.1909 †9.3.1943), a skilful goal-scoring threat in the 1932 championship team. 1 x GC

Kuffour, Samuel (*3.9.1976), rough but classy defender from Ghana (1994–2005, 175/7). 3 x DFB, 6 x GC, 1 x CL

Samuel Kuffour

Miroslav Klose liked to celebrate his goals with a somersault.

Kunstwadl, Adolf (*8.2.1940), powerful defender in the Oberliga, Regionalliga and Bundesliga

Kupferschmidt, Peter (*2.3.1942), defender who could suffer from nerves (1965–70. 135/4). 3 x DFB, 1 x GC, 1 x CWC

Kutterer, Emil (*11.11.1898 †13.7.1974), fearless left back in the 1920s

Bixente Lizarazu

L

Labbadia, Bruno (*8.2.1966), centre forward with low centre of gravity (1991–94, 82/28). 1 x GC

Lahm, Philipp (*11.11.1983), in a class of his own at full back (2005–13, 232/7). 4 x GC, 4 x DFB, 1 x CL

Laudrup, Brian (*22.2.1969), short-legged dribbler, won the European Championships with Denmark (1990–92, 53/11)

Lerby, Soren (*1.2.1958), stylish Danish midfield dynamo (1983–86, 89/22). 2 x DFB, 2 x GC

Linke, Thomas (*26.12.1969), extremely reliable defender (1998–2005, 165/2). 3 x DFB, 5 x GC, 1 x CL

Lizarazu, Bixente (*9.12.1969), small Basque player, awesome left back (1997–2006, 182/7). 5 x DFB, 6 x GC, 1 x CL

Lúcio (*8.5.1978), powerful centre back from Brazil who loved to move upfield (2004–09, 144/7). 3 x DFB, 3 x GC

M

Mai, Karl (*27.7.1928 †15.3.1993), joined from Fürth as World Cup winner (1958–61, OL: 67/2)

Maier, Sepp (*28.2.1944), funny but also enormously reliable goaltender (1965–79, 473). 4 x DFB, 4 x GC, 3 x CL, 1 x CWC

Makaay, Roy (*9.3.1975), Dutch predator with amazing scoring record (2003–07, 129/78). 2 x DFB, 2 x GC

Mandzukić, Mario (*21.5 1986), hard-working, -fighting, and -heading number 9 from Croatia (2012/13, 24/15). 1 x GC, 1 x DFB, 1 x CL

Martinez, Javier (*2.9.1988), expensive but committed Spaniard with vision (2012/13, 27/3). 1 x GC, 1 x DFB, 1 x CL

Mathy, Reinhold (*12.4.1962), never really fulfilled his promise in midfield (1980–87, 100/21). 3 x DFB, 4 x GC

Matthäus, Lothar (*21.3.1961), team leader, filibuster, world player of the year (1984–88, 1992–00, 302/85). 2 x DFB, 6 x GC, 1 x UEFA

Moll, Herbert (*13.12.1916 †10.2.2002), stylish midfielder who hardly committed a foul between 1935 and 1951

Mrosko, Karl-Heinz (*11.10.1946), long-haired student in midfield (1969–71, 50/13). 1 x DFB

Müller, Gerd (*3.11.1945), greatest goal poacher of all time (1965–79, 427/365). 4 x DFB, 4 x GC, 3 x CL, 1 x CWC

Müller, Thomas (*13.9.1989), young forward with a drive for goal, almost like the 'old' Müller (2009–13, 134/45). 2 x GC, 2 x DFB, 1 x CL

N

Nachtweih, Norbert (*4.6.1957), brilliant defender from the former GDR (1982–89, 202/20). 2 x DFB, 4 x GC

Nafziger, Rudolf (*11.8.1945), super dribbler and heartthrob (1964–68, 116/10). 2 x DFB, 1 x CWC

Nagelschmitz, Ernst (*1.5.1902 †23.5.1987), a whizz kid who played from 1920 to 1937. 1 x GC

Nerlinger, Christian (*21.3.1973), industrious worker in midfield (1993–98, 156/27). 2 x GC, 1 x UEFA

Neuer, Manuel (*27.3.1986), the undisputed number one in the German goal (2011–13, 64/0). 1 x GC, 1 x DFB, 1 x CL.

Niedermayer, Kurt (*25.11.1955), consistent defensive player (1977–82, 145/32). 1 x DFB, 3 x GC

O

Oblak, Branko (*27.5.1947), Yugoslavian midfield maestro, comfortable on the ball (1977–80, 71/5). 1 x GC

Ohlhauser, Rainer (*6.1.1941), very fine goalscorer, 207 goals from 329 matches (160/64). 3 x DFB, 1 x GC, 1 x CWC

Olić, Ivica (*14.9.1979), fighting machine from Croatia, joined from Hamburg (2009–12, 55/13). 1 x GC, 1 x DFB

Olk, Werner (*18.1.1938), captain and defender, a trained engineer (1960-70, 144/2). 3 x DFB, 1 x GC, 1 x CWC

P

Pfaff, Jean-Marie (*4.12.1953), goalkeeper from Belgium, the fans loved him (1982–88, 156). 2 x DFB, 3 x GC

Pflügler, Hans (*27.3.1960), defender who was rarely beaten (1981–1992/95, 277/36). 3 x DFB, 5 x GC

Pizarro, Claudio (*3.10.1978), the 'Pizza' from Peru, always dangerous in front of goal (2001–07, 2012/13, 194/77). 4 x GC, 4 x DFB, 1 x CL

Podolski, Lukas (*4.6.1985), a regular in the national team, but not at Bayern (2006–09, 71/15). 1 x DFB, 1 x GC

Pöttinger, Josef (*16.4.1903 †9.9.1970), nobody caressed the ball like the lad from Munich-Neuhausen, 1921–1932.

R

Rafinha (*7.9.1985), small and hot-headed full back from Brazil (2011–13, 37/2). 1 x GC, 1 x DFB, 1 x CL

Reuter, Stefan (*16.10.1966), very fast midfielder from Dinkelsbühl (1988–91, 95/4). 2 x GC

Ribéry, Franck (*7.4.1983), almost unstoppable whirlwind from France (2007–13, 156/53). 3 x GC, 3 x DFB, 1 x CL

Old trading card of Josef Pöttinger.

Even as a 16-year-old player with the Under-17s, Michael Rummenigge already knew that he wanted to become a professional like his famous brother Karl-Heinz.

Rizzitelli, Ruggiero (*2.9.1967), first Italian striker in Bayern's colours (1996–98, 45/11). 1 x DFB, 1 x GC

Robben, Arjen (*23.1.1984), can dribble past people in a phone box (2009–13, 78/45). 2 x GC, 2 x DFB, 1 x CL

Rohr, Oskar (*24.4.1912 †8.11.1988), best striker in Bayern's first champion team, 1930–32. 1 x GC

Roth, Franz (*27.4.1946), brawny midfield dynamo with a powerful shot (1966–78, 322/72). 2 x DFB, 4 x GC, 3 x CL, 1 x CWC

Rummenigge, Karl-Heinz (*22.9.1955), second best goalscorer after Gerd Müller (1974–84, 310/162). 2 x DFB, 2 x GC

Rummenigge, Michael (*3.2.1964), Karl-Heinz's kid brother in midfield (1982–88, 152/45). 2 x DFB, 3 x GC

Willy Sagnol

S

Sagnol, Willy (*18.3.1977), French world-class full back (2000–09, 184/7). 4 x DFB, 5 x GC, 1 x CL

Salihamidzic, Hasan (*1.1.1977), covered more miles than almost anyone (1998–2007, 234/30). 4 x DFB, 6 x GC, 1 x CL

Santa Cruz, Roque (*16.8.1981), teen heart-throb and talented forward (1999–2007, 155/31). 4 x DFB, 5 x GC, 1 x CL

Scholl, Mehmet (*16.10.1970), all Bayern fans loved his silky skills (1992–2007, 334/86). 5 x DFB, 8 x GC, 1 x CL, 1 x UEFA

Schupp, Markus (*7.1.1966), rather inconspicuous player from Kaiserslautern (1992–95, 91/12). 1 x GC

Schwabl, Manfred (*18.4.1966), constantly moved between Nuremberg and Munich (1984–93, 110/7). 1 x DFB, 3 x GC

Schwarzenbeck, Georg (*3.4.1948), super-reliable stopper (1966–80, 416/21). 3 x DFB, 5 x GC, 3 x CL, 1 x CWC

Schweinsteiger, Bastian (*1.8.1984), bag of tricks from Kolbermoor (2002–13, 299/36). 6 x GC, 6 x DFB, 1 x CL

Sergio, Paulo (*2.6.1969), devout Christian and forward from Brazil (1999–2002, 77/21). 1 x DFB, 2 x GC, 1 x CL

Shaqiri, Xherdan (* 10.10.1991), Kosovar Albanian dribbler with Swiss passport (2012/13, 26/4). 1 x GC, 1 x DFB, 1 x CL

Siedl, Gerhard (*22.3.1929 †9.5.1998), exceptional forward in the 1950s (OL: 132/35)

Simetsreiter, Wilhelm (*6.3.1915 †17.7.2001), great Bayern forward up to the Oberliga era (1934–47)

Sternkopf, Michael (*21.4.1970), long-haired talent from Karlsruhe who never broke through (1990–95, 94/4). 1 x GC

Streitle, Jakob (*11.12.1916 †24.6.1982), captain and defender from 1935 to 1955 (OL: 214/1)

Strunz, Thomas (*25.4.1968), defender, spent some time at Stuttgart (1989–2001, 235/24). 2 x DFB, 5 x GC, 1 x CL, 1 x UEFA

T

Tarnat, Michael (*27.10.1969), left-sided defensive player with a ferocious shot (1997–2003, 122/8). 3 x DFB, 4 x GC, 1 x CL

Thon, Olaf (*1.5.1966), street footballer in midfield, joined from Schalke (1988–94, 148/30). 3 x GC

Toni, Luca (*26.5.1977), Italian goalscorer, World Cup winner, ladies' man (2007–09, 60/38). 1 x GC, 1 x DFB

Torstensson, Conny (*28.8.1949), Swedish forward who wore red shoes (1973–77, 81/11). 1 x GC, 3 x CL

Tymoshchuk, Anatoliy (*30.3.1979), blond Ukrainian sweeper in front of the backline (2009–13, 86/4). 2 x GC, 2 x DFB, 1 x CL

V

Van Bommel, Mark (*22.4.1977), extremely valuable competitor from Holland (2006–11, 123/11). 2 x GC, 2 x DFB

Van Buyten, Daniel (*7.2.1978), the 'rock' in Bayern's defence (2006–13, 146/19). 3 x GC, 3 x DFB, 1 x CL

W

Wegmann, Jürgen (*31.3.1964), forward who was known as 'the cobra' (1987–89, 58/26). 1 x GC

Weiner, Hans (*29.11.1950), reliable defender known as 'Hanne from Berlin' (1979–82, 91/2). 2 x GC

Welker, Hans (*21.8.1907 †24.7.1968), homegrown winger who was national champion in 1932. 1 x GC

Witeczek, Marcel (*18.10.68), flexible and hard-working stand-in (1993–97, 97/9). 2 x GC, 1 x UEFA

Wohlfarth, Roland (*11.1.1963), consistent goalscorer for nine long years (1984–93, 254/119). 1 x DFB, 5 x GC

Wouters, Jan (*17.7.1960), hard, experienced defender from the Netherlands (1992–93, 66/6)

Z

Zé Roberto (*6.7.1974), slight and elegant Brazilian who could do anything with the ball (2002–09, 169/14). 4 x DFB, 4 x GC

Zickler, Alexander (*28.2.1974), forward with a decathlete's physique (1993–2005, 213/51). 3 x DFB, 7 x GC, 1 x CL, 1 x UEFA

Ziege, Christian (*1.2.1972), midfielder with a drive for goal (1990–97, 185/37). 2 x GC, 1 x UEFA

Zobel, Rainer (*3.11.1948), tireless runner in the successful team of the 1970s (1970–76, 180/19). 1 x DFB, 3 x GC, 3 x CL

Luca Toni

Record players

The most appearances for Bayern in the Bundesliga: Sepp Maier (473), Oliver Kahn (429), Gerd Müller (427), Georg Schwarzenbeck (416), Klaus Augenthaler (404), Franz Beckenbauer (396), Bernd Dürnberger (375), Mehmet Scholl (334), Franz Roth (322), Karl-Heinz Rummenigge (310), Lothar Matthäus (302), Bastian Schweinsteiger (299).

In the Oberliga (pre-Bundesliga era): Hans Bauer (226), Thomas Mayer (163), Jakob Streitle (160).

In Europe: Oliver Kahn (130), Klaus Augenthaler, Bastian Schweinsteiger (89), Mehmet Scholl, Hasan Salihamidzic (88), Sepp Maier, Bernd Dürnberger (78), Philipp Lahm (77), Gerd Müller, Samuel Kuffour (74), Franz Beckenbauer (71), Georg Schwarzenbeck (70).

Lots of young boys have a dream of one day playing professional football for Bayern Munich. The path to get there is long and difficult. Only a few end up wearing the famous red shirt in the Bundesliga and Champions League. Many successful pros, including Philipp Lahm and Bastian Schweinsteiger, already played for Bayern at the youth level. The club's youth set-up is still a good place to start. Every Bayern youth team, however, plays at the very top level, and only the very best kids manage to break into one of these teams.

The best opportunity to get yourself noticed is the annual TALENT Day. Information for the written application can be found under www.fcbayern.telekom.de/de/mannschaften/junior/info. (Please note: due to the huge number of enquiries, not every applicant can be considered!)

You do not have to live in Munich in order to be able to register for the TALENT Day, which usually takes place in July at the Säbener Strasse grounds. In principle, young talent from all over the world can take part in this scouting tournament. All Bayern Munich coaches watch the kids and then select their favourites. The best will be called up to the junior team's youngest side.

This is what happened in 2013: Those born between 2003 and 2006 were allowed to apply. Around 500 kids were approved. Every participant was then permitted to take part in a mini tournament (five-a-side) for three games, each lasting 20 minutes. The junior team coaches, led by former pros Wolfgang Dremmler and Michael Tarnat, then conferred. And a short time later, the best players received an invitation to a trial training session.

Aside from the TALENT Days, every summer FC Bayern together with the Hans Dorfner Football Academy holds lots of football camps. And these are not just held at the Säbener Strasse grounds. In 2013 there were camps such as these in, for example, Trentino (Italy), in the Europa-Park in Rust, in Bochum, in Salzburg (Austria) and in Herzogenaurauch. More detailed information and the registration forms for the separate camps can be found under www.fcbayern.telekom.de/kidsclub/fussballcamp.php (German-language only). If too many children apply, participants will be chosen at random.

Föttinger, Bayern - München

AMMELWETTBEWERB
ihe A
k-Nr. 0586637
aufbewahren. Bitte, Rückseite beachten.